❦ Samuel Adams ❦

Samuel Adams

SON OF LIBERTY

CLIFFORD LINDSEY ALDERMAN

Holt, Rinehart and Winston
New York · Chicago · San Francisco

For Ricky Waldron

∽ Samuel Adams ∾

Chapter I

BACK IN THE time of our Revolution the Tories in the American colonies who remained loyal to England called him the Chief Incendiary because he lighted a fire of independence in the hearts and minds of the people. It was just a spark at first. Samuel Adams tended it throughout his life, fanning it when it smoldered and almost died out, building it up until at last it burst into the raging flame of the American Revolution.

Samuel Adams never gave up, even though at times he had to fight alone when other great patriots wavered. There were many who felt that it would be foolhardy for the sparsely settled, weak colonies to oppose the powerful, rich mother country, and that it would be better for the people to remain subjects of the British Empire. But as a young man, Samuel Adams became convinced that the American colonies must win their independence. From then until the Revolution was over, he devoted all his energies to that cause.

If we look at a copy of the Declaration of Independence, the first name we notice among the fifty-six signatures at the bottom is that of John Hancock. It is written in a large, bold, even hand, adorned with scrolls and flourishes. Samuel Adams' signature is there, too, but the writing is small and insignificant, the faltering script betraying the palsy from which he suffered throughout most of his life. Yet his name belongs with those of such great patriots as Thomas Jefferson, John Adams, and Benjamin Franklin, for the Declaration of Independence might not have been written in 1776, or perhaps ever, but for Samuel Adams.

How did it happen that this man worked so tirelessly, so persistently, for American liberty? What first gave him the idea that the colonies should be free of English rule? The answers to these questions are to be found in the story of his life—and it is an exciting story, full of intrigue, mysteries, and violence. Yet it begins in a quite ordinary way, with no hint of the future role he was to play in shaping the destiny of this country.

Samuel Adams was born at noon on September 16, 1722. Still, it was not too late in the day to carry the newborn baby to the New South Church to be baptized. His mother, Mary Adams, a woman of strict religious principles, could take no chances. If her infant son should die before they got him to the church, he would go to hell and burn forever in its flaming fires; so said the church of the Puritans. Thus it was that Captain Samuel Adams and his wife and child started out from their large home on Purchase Street in the South End of Boston that same afternoon.

Captain Adams had built the house for his bride before their marriage in 1713. It was close to the water-front and afforded a magnificent view of Boston Harbor. A flight of steps led up the outside of the house to a platform, or captain's walk, on top of the roof, and from there one could see all the way out to the open sea. Many Boston houses had these platforms so that sea captains' wives could watch for their husbands' return.

Captain Adams was not a shipmaster, however. He had earned his title as a militia officer during the long series of wars that Massachusetts Bay and other American colonies fought against the Indians and their French allies to the north in Canada. He was a prosperous brewer, and the malthouse where he made beer and ale stood on his property not far from the house.

It was only a short distance down Purchase Street to the Church Green at Summer Street and Blind Lane. In his mother's arms, Sam may have squalled lustily in the church, but it did him no good. The Reverend Samuel Checkley duly baptized the infant to save his tiny soul.

Sam was the fourth child to be born to the Adamses, but only one other, a daughter, had lived beyond babyhood, for in those days babies often died shortly after birth. Mary was then five, old enough to do things for herself and to start learning to help her mother with the household tasks. Mrs. Adams had her hands full taking care of little Sam and cooking, baking pies and bread, and spinning and weaving flax and wool into warm garments for her family.

When Sam was old enough to go out and play with other boys, he discovered that there were all sorts of exciting things to see and do. For one thing, there were the wharves. Tall ships were moored there, in from their voyages. Sam Adams and his playmates gaped in awe at the busy, bronzed, pigtailed sailors, with their wide-flared breeches and their bright-colored kerchiefs bound around their heads. Some might be hard at work unloading casks, chests, and bales. Other seamen might be hoisting cargo aboard another vessel: lumber, barrel staves, and casks of dried codfish bound for distant ports. When the holds were full, the crew would scuttle like monkeys into the rigging and loose the sails. Then, as the captain bawled hoarse orders, the lines would be cast off, and the ship would move slowly out of the harbor like a ponderous white-winged bird. The boys would watch until she disappeared from view, longing for the day when they, too, would be sailors and sail away to far places.

The end of a wharf was a favorite spot on a hot summer's day—the perfect place for diving into the cool, sparkling water. Most boys in Boston learned to swim before they were much bigger than tadpoles. And Sam soon discovered that by dropping a baited hook and line into the bay he could quickly haul in a nice string of the little mackerel that swarmed there in schools, or scoons as they were called.

The ropewalks were just a few steps up the long slope that rose gradually from the harbor to the heart of town. There, in a shed so long that the other end was scarcely visible, Sam and his companions would watch a man walk slowly backward, holding the end of a new rope that grew longer and longer as another man at the big spinning wheel in the front part of the shed twisted

4

fibers and spun them into cordage for ships' anchor cable and other purposes.

The blacksmiths' shops were fascinating places, too. Fires leaped up under the blast of the bellows, lighting up the gloomy interior and casting eerie shadows over the sweaty face of the smith as he drew bar after bar of glowing, cherry-red metal from the forge. The muscles in his bare arms and shoulders would ripple, and the anvil would clang as he swung his hammer, fashioning horseshoes and other iron objects.

The peninsula on which Boston stood was far from built up, and there were many fields and pastures where Sam and his friends could fly kites and play games. There was one-old-cat, which was much like baseball, and a kind of football; there was blindman's buff, leapfrog, hopscotch, and marbles. They also played other games whose names are strange to us—chuck-farthing, stool-ball, tip-cat, fives, thread-the-needle, woo-the-widow, and hoop-and-hide—but which were very much like the games children play today.

In winter the boys whizzed down hills on sleds or double rippers, which were made from a plank and two sleds and were similar to our bobsleds. They suffered their share of broken arms and legs, bumps, bruises, and bloody noses but, like all boys everywhere, were undeterred by such mishaps. After a heavy snowfall rival armies from the North and South Ends would build huge snow forts on the Common and wage fierce snowball battles until dusk sent them scurrying to warm firesides.

Every Sabbath, Sam's parents saw to it that he attended the New South Church, where Captain Adams was a deacon. In Boston in those days people went to the meetinghouse even if a blizzard was raging, and it was almost as cold inside as it was outside.

Sam sat in the gallery, a place specially set aside for boys, where the tithing man could keep an eye on them and be ready to give mischief-makers a rap with his tithing rod. Despite that ever-present threat of chastisement, the restless boys wriggled, giggled, and whispered. Now and then a boy would manage to smuggle a dog into church. Or another might bend down out of sight, put a blade of grass between his thumbs, and blow on it. The ear-splitting screech that resulted would bring the tithing man on the run and cause the minister to pause in his sermon and frown up at the gallery.

Mary Adams, being so devout, had hopes that her son would become a minister. But that lay far in the future, and Sam began his education at one of the Boston dame schools. These schools were so called because they were usually run by an elderly spinster or widow who needed to earn her living. All too often it proved to be no easy job, for discipline was difficult to maintain among unruly boys who were forever dreaming up pranks to harry these poor, long-suffering ladies.

There is no evidence that Sam Adams was involved in classroom escapades. But he was no sissy, though a serious-minded youngster, and it is more than likely that he did his share to make the schooldame's life miserable. At any rate, he studied his ABC's from the hornbook and learned to read and write from the *New England Primer*.

The hornbook was not a book but a flat slab of wood with a handle, shaped much like a square hand mirror. Pasted on it was a sheet of paper containing the letters of the alphabet. To keep it from being soiled by grimy little fingers, it was covered with a transparent sheet of horn. The *New England Primer,* a small book of about eighty pages, had verses, each beginning with a letter of the alphabet. Most of the verses were taken from Bible stories, and each had a picture to go with it. It also had exercises for reading and copying and a catechism with over a hundred questions and answers about the Bible and religion.

At the age of seven Sam was ready for public school. There were five of them in Boston, some called grammar schools, others known as writing-schools. Both kinds were for boys only, since education for girls beyond dame school was considered unnecessary. Because he was preparing for Harvard College, Sam went to the Boston Latin School.

Boston Latin stood, quite appropriately, on School Street. It was a two-story building with a gambrel, or dog-leg, roof, and a belfry. In the classrooms the scholars sat on wooden benches. There was no tuition, but each boy had to pay a "firing fee" for the wood that was burned to heat the school in cold weather.

Today it is hard to imagine a seven-year-old studying Latin, but Sam Adams did. In fact, Latin was the principal subject taught at the school. One of the Latin textbooks used at that time was entitled *A delysious Syrupe newly Clarified for Yonge Scholars that thurste for the Swete Lycore of Latin Speche.* How

7

thirsty Sam was for that sweet liquor is not recorded, but since he was graduated he must have gotten plenty of it. In his first three years at the school he had to memorize several books in Latin. One was Aesop's Fables, which he later had to turn into Latin verse. He was also required to study Greek and read the works of famous Roman and Greek poets, writers, and historians. In addition, he spent an hour each day learning penmanship and arithmetic.

The school hours were long and the discipline strict. When the students were tardy, did not know their lessons, played hookey, were inattentive or whispered in class, cheated, or used bad language, Nathaniel Williams, the schoolmaster, would chastise them with a short, stubby rod called a ferrule. But Sam Adams seems to have been a model scholar. He was certainly not tardy, for the workmen he saw on his way to and from school said they could set their watches by his passing.

By this time Sam was old enough to understand the discussions between his parents at home. Captain Adams, like many other colonials, was interested in politics and government. Often after supper he would put on his hat and say to his wife, "I'm going to the Two Palaverers, my dear. The Caulkers Club is meeting."

Sam knew the Two Palaverers, for in his ramblings he had often passed it, a snug tavern near the North End waterfront. Because of the sign that hung over its door showing two courtly gentlemen bowing and scraping to each other, its real name was the Salutation Tavern, but no one used anything but the nickname someone had bestowed upon it. As for the Caulkers Club, Sam knew what that was, too—his father and some other men had organized it. When the day's work was over, shipyard workers would drift into the taproom of the Two Palaverers to spend the evening discussing colonial problems and politics over a mug of flip or small beer. The club had gotten its name because many of its members were caulkers, as well as shipwrights, gravers, sparmakers, and others in the shipbuilding trade. Today, a political meeting is often called a "caucus," which may be a corruption of the word "caulkers."

After a meeting Captain Adams would tell his wife about what had been said. "We discussed the governor's salary last night," he said one morning at breakfast. "Jonnie Belcher'd better have a care. He knows what happened to Sam Shute."

Young Sam's eyes widened when he heard his father refer to Governor Jonathan Belcher as "Jonnie." The name always brought to mind Visitation Day, when the governor had come to the Boston Latin School.

What a furor of preparation preceded that visit! Brooms were plied vigorously, and inkstains on the floor were scrubbed off. After sharpening the quill pens, the boys filled the inkstands. The neatest and most ornamental of the scholars' copybooks were then put out for the honored guest's inspection.

Master Lovell, who had succeeded Master Williams, was nervous and flustered. He posted Sam at the schoolroom window, ordering, "Let me know the instant you see the governor's coach approaching."

At last the shiny black vehicle, aglitter with gilding, turned the corner. "They're coming!" Sam cried.

"Let me know when His Excellency gets out!" Master Lovell quavered.

As soon as the coach came to a halt in front of the schoolhouse, footmen in livery leaped down to open its door. A procession of other carriages rolled up behind it.

"He's getting down!" Sam called out in a raucous whisper and scurried back to his seat.

Outside, the tramp of feet grew louder as Master Lovell's assistants, known as ushers, approached and then flung open the school door with a flourish. At Lovell's nod the scholars rose, standing at stiff attention but with their mouths gaping as if they were all trying to catch flies.

Sam stared at the tall, aristocratic-looking figure in a tightly laced scarlet coat heavy with gold lace, white satin waistcoat, and scarlet breeches. He was astounded at the great powdered wig the governor was wearing. A sword flashed at his side as he entered the classroom, followed by Lieutenant Governor Spencer Phips and the head of the Visitation Committee. Next came the governor's Council and his staff, representatives of the General Court, the selectmen of Boston, a black-robed minister or two, and, last, several doctors, lawyers, and overseers of the poor.

Master Lovell gave a sweeping bow, bending so low that Sam feared he would fall on his face. The ushers fluttered about, showing the bigwigs to their seats at the head of the schoolroom. When everyone was settled, Master Lovell saluted His Excellency with a Latin oration of welcome; the governor responded, also in Latin.

The visit was not as dreadful as Sam had feared it would be. The scholars read passages in Latin, translated them into English, translated English to Latin. The copybooks were shown the governor, then handed about among the notables. His Excellency asked a few questions, but he beamed benignly and Master Lovell visibly relaxed a little. When it was all over, the governor gave the whole school a holiday.

Nevertheless, it had been an awesome occasion. So when Captain Adams called the governor Jonnie, Sam was somewhat startled. Still, he told himself, there was really nothing so strange about it. His father was an important man himself. Captain Adams was among the guests at school that day, for he was one of the selectmen who governed the town of Boston, just as they have selectmen today in New England villages too small to have a mayor.

There was another reason why Captain Adams could speak so familiarly of the governor.

"Why should Jonnie Belcher be uppish?" he said to his wife. "Born right here in Boston, wasn't he? I may be a little older than he is, but I remember him well as a boy. We thought when the King chose a man born in Massachusetts Bay as royal governor we'd get along with him."

"But why shouldn't the colony pay him, Samuel?" Mrs. Adams asked her husband during one of the discussions about the governor's salary.

"Why should we?" Sam's father snapped. "We

didn't elect him. The King appointed him—let the Crown pay him. Besides, the General Court's offered him a thousand pounds a year, but only for this year. Belcher demands a regular salary."

"But if he's to be paid by the colony, hasn't he a right to a regular salary?" Mrs. Adams persisted. "How does he know the General Court won't change its mind next year and refuse to pay him anything?"

"That's just it!" Captain Adams replied. "That's the only way we can make sure he won't become a tyrant like Andros. If he tries it, we'll refuse to pay him."

Captain Adams had often talked of Sir Edmund Andros, the colony's first royal governor long before Sam was born. Now he spoke of those days again.

"You know how it was before Andros, my dear," he told his wife. "Under the old charter we had freedom. Of course, we were loyal subjects of the King, but we chose our own governors and made our own laws. Ever since Charles II took away the charter, however, the King has appointed our governors, who approve all the laws we wish to make."

Sometimes, when the previous night's discussion at the Caulkers Club had been particularly heated, Captain Adams would speak of how the people of Massachusetts Bay had risen in revolt, seized the tyrant Andros, and put him in prison. Then they had sent him to London to be tried.

"It could happen again," he would say darkly. "We're Englishmen, and Englishmen stand up for their rights. The English people have driven more than one king from the throne when he became a tyrant. Why should we have a royal governor set over us? Why should he say what laws we can make? In England the people make their own laws in the Parliament. When an Englishman's rights are taken from him he asserts his independence. When driven to it we must assert *ours*."

Independence . . . that was something new to young Sam. He had not known that more than once the people of England had risen against their kings. It made an impression on him that he never forgot, and as he grew older he thought about it more and more. People had rights. If those rights were taken away, they could rise and assert their independence. . . .

Sam learned from his father that there had been a similar dispute over Governor Samuel Shute's salary. When the leaders of the colony had sent a complaint to the King and asked him to recall Shute, George I had done so and sent a new governor. Later, when a similar complaint was made against Jonathan Belcher, King George II recalled him, too.

In the spring of 1736 Sam Adams, now thirteen years old, delivered an oration in Latin before the Boston Latin School, an event that marked his graduation. At last he was ready for the great adventure of Harvard College.

⚬ Chapter 2 ⚬

TODAY HARVARD IS a large, rich university, with many buildings and thousands of students. Although it had been America's first college and was one hundred years old in 1736, it was still small. There were but three buildings, and Sam Adams' class numbered only twenty-two members.

At a time when many people kept diaries, Sam—who probably wrote more words in his lifetime than any other man in the American colonies—set down very little about himself; therefore we know little about his college years. Nevertheless, we know many things that must have happened to him, since all Harvard students experienced them.

In the summer of 1736 Sam journeyed across the Charles River to Cambridge, where he faced President Benjamin Wadsworth and the college tutors for his entrance examination. It proved to be a solemn ordeal; in Old Harvard Hall he was questioned on everything he had learned. But being well prepared, he was admitted as a freshman in the class of 1740.

The quarters to which he was assigned, along with

several other young men, consisted of one large, comfortably furnished room, with a tiny compartment for each occupant to use as a study.

We do not know who Sam's roommates were. Most of the students came from Boston or other Massachusetts Bay towns, but there were always a few from the New York colony. These "foreigners," as they were called, were usually the sons of wealthy men. They had their London magazines and their books of plays, which members of the Puritan sect had been taught to consider scandalous, as was anything connected with the theater. They brought their own tea sets, chafing dishes, mirrors, and pictures. They had crimping irons for curling their wigs; their expensive clothes came from London.

Since his father was well off, Sam, too, could have afforded such luxuries, but he had been brought up in a Puritan home and probably scorned them. Nevertheless, he did live very comfortably.

In each room where there were freshmen it was customary to assign a graduate student preparing for his master's degree. With everything so new and strange to them, Sam and his roommates had to look to this wise and experienced authority for guidance.

"Go over to Commons in Old Harvard and see Andrew Boardman, the steward," must have been the first instructions of the bachelor, as a graduate student was called. "He'll post you in the Buttery as a member of the House. You'd better see the butler, too, about your bever."

How Sam and his classmates must have stared.

Commons . . . the House . . . the Buttery . . . bever . . . ? What strange talk was this? But not wanting to show their ignorance, they went to Harvard Hall and inquired for Mr. Boardman.

The steward turned out to be an imposing personage who ruled over the Commons, which turned out to be the students' dining hall. They paid Mr. Boardman a shilling apiece to be posted as members of the House, the students' name for Harvard College.

Next, they met the butler, who supervised the Buttery. This consisted of a kitchen, a sort of general store, and an office where students' attendance records were kept. The butler tended the store, kept the records, and rang the bell in the belfry for rising, going to bed, and attendance at prayers and meals. He also saw to it that Old Harvard was swept out and cleaned and that the cook kept his utensils properly scoured.

"You'll be issued bever twice a day at the Buttery hatch," he told the freshmen. When they looked puzzled, he explained, "Bever is breakfast and a late afternoon snack—two sizings and a cue. You'll be wanting extra provisions like the rest, I suppose. I sell them in the store."

What sizings and cues were, Sam and his new friends did not learn until afternoon, when they and all the other students each drew two slabs of bread and a mug of beer at the Buttery hatch. Breakfast the next morning was the same. As for the extra provisions the butler had mentioned, it seemed strange. Since their tuition was supposed to cover all meals, why should they have to buy more food?

16

That evening they found out when their bachelor roommate escorted them over to Commons for supper. The uproar in the big room was deafening as the students came charging in, all talking at once, pushing and jostling for the best seats. The bachelor, Sam, and the others finally managed to find empty places at one of the tables.

Although the tutors at Harvard College always used the term, "young gentlemen," the students had atrocious table manners. Everywhere Sam looked, upperclassmen were howling for food and beating on the table tops with their knives and forks, which they had brought to Commons with them. As soon as a large platter of bread was set down, there was such a mad scramble for the sizings that Sam was barely able to snatch one before the platter was empty.

At his elbow, the bachelor said, "Pin it down, Adams. Like this." Laying the slice of bread on the table, he drove the point of his knife through it into the wood. "They'll steal anything that isn't nailed down," he explained.

There was another noisy scuffle as huge platters of meat were served, but this time Sam was alert to the need for swift action and a long reach. He skewered a slab of meat with his fork and began to eat, noticing that it had a peculiar taste, as if it had been kept a little too long. Others in the dining hall noticed it too, and set up a furious howl:

"The meat's spoiled! Get President Wadsworth in here! Make him eat it! Then maybe we'll get something besides swill!"

In spite of all the complaints, the meat vanished in no time. When it and the bread were gone, the students banged and clamored for more. But a tutor had risen, holding up his hand for silence, and gradually the din subsided. During the tutor's prayer of thanks for the food, the students wiped their knives and forks clean on the tablecloths and afterward swarmed out of the Commons.

Before Sam had been at Harvard many days, he began to see why the butler made a handsome profit selling extra delicacies at the Buttery. Like most young men, the students had voracious appetites. And, if the quality of the food in Commons was not high, the quantity always seemed to fall short, too. In fact, groups of students were known to sneak out of quarters in the middle of the night to raid a neighboring barnyard. Then, back in their rooms, they would stuff themselves with the chicken, duck, or goose they had roasted in their fireplaces. It went hard with those who were caught, but that did not stop the midnight feasts.

If Sam was a little homesick at first—even though he was able to visit his family now and then—he was soon too busy to pine for the boyhood days on Purchase Street. Not only did his studies take up much time, but tradition forced other duties upon freshmen at Harvard.

One day early in the school year the entire first-year class was summoned to Old Harvard, where a sophomore addressed them: "We have certain customs here at Harvard which all freshmen must obey without question. Fail to do so at your peril." He looked around at his audience with a menacing scowl. "Always remember that you are freshmen and that a freshman is lower than a dog."

After an effective pause the speaker continued: "You will carry out all orders given you by your betters. An order from an upperclassman is to be obeyed instantly. However, the command of a senior sophister must be obeyed before you carry out the order of a junior sophister. In the same way a junior sophister's command takes precedence over a sophomore's."

Then the freshmen were thoroughly instructed as to what customs they must observe. After that Sam and his classmates were careful to keep their hats off in the Yard. They always let their betters have the railing side when they met on a stairway. They never yelled to each other in the corridors; at prayers they stood erect and motionless.

Shortly after that meeting Sam and his roommates were in their quarters when a loud knock sounded at the door. Obedient to custom, Sam leaped up and opened it. A senior sophister stood there with a piece of paper in his hand. He looked hard at one of Sam's roommates. "Take this note to Wilkins, the junior sophister, in Stoughton Hall," he directed. "Wait for an answer."

As the freshman scurried off, the senior turned to Sam. "You, Adams," he said, "will in the future run down to the Buttery at the rising bell each morning and fetch me my sizings and cue. At the first stroke of the bell, mark you. And remember, I said *run*."

Sam carried out this and other commands obediently, living for the wonderful day when he would be a sophomore and could give orders to the new freshman class of 1741. He, too, carried notes, ran errands, took clothes to be pressed. He toted bats, balls, and footballs between the Buttery where they were kept and the "play-space" where the lordly upper classmen enjoyed their games. Betweentimes Sam was hard at work learning more Latin and Greek and studying rhetoric. When the time came to harvest President Wadsworth's hay, the first-year students did the job.

Toward the end of Sam's freshman year an important change took place in Cambridge; Wadsworth died and Edward Holyoke, a tutor at Harvard as well as its librarian, was elected president of the college. There was no doubt about it—Mr. Holyoke liked the students, and they in turn liked him. Instinctively they trusted this man, and he did not let them down.

Commencement at Harvard was always a great event. Strangely enough, at this college, which had been founded by stern Puritans who frowned on merrymaking, Commencement was a riotous day of revelry in which everyone from the governor down to paupers, beggars, and thieves took part. Of course there were a few blue-nosed prigs who frowned upon such high jinks, and one of them even offered the college a gift of one thousand pounds on condition that the shameless goings-on at Commencement be ended.

President Holyoke refused the gift, saying in substance, "The boys have a right to celebrate one day a year."

"Huzza for Holyoke!" the students shouted. "He's got guts!" And after that the president was known to every Harvard undergraduate as "Guts" Holyoke.

The end of that first year came at last, and Sam was ranked fifth in his class of twenty-two students. Today, scholastic ability determines class standing, but at Harvard in those days it had nothing to do with marks. There were none anyway; a student either passed or he didn't. Instead, his class standing depended upon how important his father was—how much money he had, what kind of position he held. That Sam stood fifth shows how important Captain Adams was in Boston.

Sam spent the summer vacation at home. Even though he was still planning to be a minister, he took a lively interest in politics, and it is more than likely that he went to several meetings of the Caulkers Club with his father.

Captain Adams told his son about some ambitious plans that he and several of the other leading men of the colony were working out.

"The colony has never had much money," he told Sam, "but we're going to change that."

Captain Adams was right about the money, and the problem stemmed from the fact that Massachusetts Bay's wealth depended largely upon trade and commerce with England. Colonial women spun their own yarn, wove it into cloth, and made their own clothes. Most of the food was raised on their farms; many household and other small articles were made in America. But almost everything else, tools, plows, fine cloth, chinaware, bricks, and other materials, had to be imported from the mother country. There were wealthy merchants who were able to pay for such merchandise in hard coin, but farmers and townspeople either went without or got into debt buying from the merchants. If such colonial products as lumber, barrel staves, whale oil, fish, and fur skins could have been exported to foreign markets, it would have been possible to accumulate and circulate more currency. However, strict English laws forbade trade except with England and the other British colonies.

"How are you going to change the situation?" Sam asked his father.

"We're going to issue paper money," Captain Adams replied. "We're starting a bank to do it."

Sam knew little about money and cared less, but he did know that a person couldn't just open a bank and start printing paper money.

"Any currency a bank issues will be worthless unless there's capital back of it, gold or silver," he pointed out.

But the older man shook his head in disagreement. "Those of us who are starting the bank all own land. Land is as good as hard money. We'll put up our property as security for the paper bills we print. That's why we're going to call it the Land Bank. We'll make loans to people who put up their land and they'll spend the money; that way there'll be more in circulation."

The idea sounded all right to Sam. After all, a lot of prominent men would be among the bank's directors. His father would probably become one of Boston's most prosperous citizens.

Back at Harvard that fall, Sam took up logic, natural philosophy, divinity, and Hebrew. After attending lectures on these subjects, he went to Old Harvard twice a week to discuss with other students what he had learned.

The second year passed uneventfully, as did the third, when Sam began the study of physics, ethics, geography, and metaphysics. One welcome change took place, however. Junior sophisters were allowed to dine outside the Yard if they could afford it. Sam decided to end his days of battling for food in Commons and began to board with a family in Cambridge.

Unfortunately, no portrait of Samuel Adams as a Harvard student exists. In those days, usually only the sons and daughters of nobility or the very rich had their portraits painted. In later years, however, several artists, including the famous John Singleton Copley, painted his portrait, and from these we can get some idea of how he looked as a college student. His eyes were dark blue, kindly, serious, and compelling. For the rest, we can picture him as a well-set-up young man of medium height, with a high, broad forehead, firm mouth, and determined chin. The bushy eyebrows that are so noticeable in the paintings were probably not as pronounced when he was younger.

Sam finally began his senior year. In addition to the subjects he had started earlier, he took up two new ones, geometry and astronomy. At night he explored the mysteries of the heavens through a twenty-four-inch telescope given by one of Harvard's great benefactors, Thomas Hollis, a London merchant.

During this time Sam met a member of the new freshman class of 1743 who was to be his friend for many years and who would become a famous though hot-headed patriot. James Otis was a big, thickset, bull-necked young fellow from Cape Cod. In spite of his size, his movements were quick and jerky, and he had a hot temper. And since he loved to dispute with others, it is almost certain that Sam Adams, who also loved a good argument, enjoyed many a spirited debate with Otis on the political questions that interested both intensely.

As graduation approached, a street of tents went up in the Yard. It must have resembled a carnival midway, with all kinds of food and drink being sold, freaks exhibited, puppet shows and other forms of amusement offered. The day before graduation, clouds of dust arose from every road leading to Cambridge as an endless cavalcade of vehicles approached. Every available room in the taverns and private homes was sold out.

Despite the revelry in the tents, the Commencement ceremony was a solemn event. It was held in the meetinghouse in Cambridge, and every dignitary from the governor to the lowliest official who could possibly squeeze in was present. Captain and Mrs. Adams were undoubtedly among the proud parents who also attended.

First, a grave and silent procession of the graduates, headed by the president and the fellows, overseers, and tutors of the college, made its way from the Yard to the church. There followed a great deal of oratory in Latin, and then the members of the class of 1740 filed up to the lectern, where President Holyoke conferred bachelor's degrees upon them.

But the biggest event of the day was the dinner that followed in Old Harvard. Practically everyone in Massachusetts Bay with any pretensions to prominence was invited. The graduating class paid for the dinner, a sumptuous affair that cost each student more than a whole year's tuition at Harvard. Fortunately, Sam did not have to worry, for Captain Adams could afford it. The Land Bank had been organized. All over Massachusetts Bay, people had pledged their property as security for loans of the paper money the bank had printed. It was a time of prosperity for the Adams family.

There were many speeches at the dinner. The guests ate heartily and thoroughly enjoyed themselves while outside, in the Yard, the merrymaking in the tents went on. Some of the revelers became tipsy; inevitably there were wrestling matches and a few fist fights. But at last it was over. Notables and riffraff alike went home. The owners of the tents took them down and vanished for another year. Only heaps of rubbish, watermelon rind, peach stones, and empty bottles remained as evidence of Sam Adams' graduation day.

He was not through with Harvard, however. He was now a junior bachelor and a candidate for a master's degree. It would take him three more years to get it.

It is not known exactly when Sam Adams gave up his plan to become a minister, but it was some time during this period. He decided instead to be a lawyer. His mother was greatly disappointed, for like many religious people, she would have derived great pride and satisfaction from having a minister in the family. But Sam, who had done much reading at Harvard, had discovered that many of the great political figures were lawyers, and politics interested Sam more than anything else.

And then, in the spring of 1741, Sam Adams' whole world collapsed. One day he went to Boston to see his family, and as soon as he entered the house on Purchase Street, he sensed that something was wrong. When he embraced his mother she said nothing, but her face was grave. And as he shook hands with his father, the older man did not meet his son's gaze.

"Come into the sitting room, Samuel," Captain Adams said. "There is something I must tell you."

The elder Adams bade his son be seated, but he himself remained standing. As he spoke he paced back and forth, his brow furrowed and his eyes dull with despair and anxiety.

"The Land Bank has failed, my son," Captain Adams announced abruptly.

Sam was startled, but as yet he had no idea of what his father's words would mean to him and the entire Adams family.

"Don't worry, Father," he said cheerfully. "It doesn't mean the end of the world. You still have the brewery. Besides, you're an important man in Boston, a selectman. . . ."

"I'm afraid you don't understand, Samuel," his father interrupted. "The paper money issued by the bank was loaned to people and went into circulation as they spent it. Now the Parliament in London has passed a law forbidding us to operate the Land Bank. That makes our currency worthless. The people who have paper bills are demanding that we redeem them with hard money. Since we do not have it, they will try to take the property the directors of the bank have pledged as security, my brewery, this house. . . ."

Captain Adams stopped pacing and faced his son squarely.

"It means that I am ruined," he said.

Chapter 3

How DID IT happen that in faraway London the Parliament had passed a law to put the Land Bank out of business? That was the next question Sam Adams asked his father.

"Governor Belcher wrote to England demanding an act of Parliament to force us to suspend our operations," Captain Adams explained. "He called the bank a vile scheme."

A vile scheme it was not, for those who had started the Land Bank were upright men. They honestly believed that what they were doing would make Massachusetts Bay and its people prosperous. But they were wrong. The principle of the Land Bank was unsound.

The trouble was that land is not money. It may be valuable, but ordinarily it cannot be used to buy things. If it is sold, the money received can be spent, of course, but it is not always easy to sell land, especially such a large amount as the Land Bank had in place of capital.

The Land Bank could not be permitted to go on printing paper money because its value would have steadily diminished as the people realized that they could not redeem it for equivalent amounts of gold or silver coin. As more and more people lost confidence in the bank's money, no one would accept the bills at their face value and the paper would eventually be worth little or nothing.

"Governor Belcher was influenced by our rich merchants," Captain Adams told his son, adding bitterly, "especially the Hutchinsons."

Wealthy Boston merchants had been against the Land Bank proposition from the very beginning, and with good reason. They had built their fortunes on the sea trade, which provided the only source of money in the colony. Naturally they did not want to share the handsome profits with their smaller competitors, who would have been able to expand their business if there was more money in circulation. True, the big merchants did not think the Land Bank could succeed, but they did not care to risk even a small possibility that it might do so, no matter how briefly.

Even more enthusiastic than the small businessmen were the farmers, who almost never had any money but owned plenty of land. When it was learned that Governor Belcher was trying to put the bank out of business, these farmers grew very angry. Five thousand of them planned a march on Boston to demand that the bank be allowed to continue. When the governor heard of the plan, he had the leaders arrested and put in jail. That stopped the march.

The Hutchinsons, of whom Captain Adams had spoken, belonged to the mercantile aristocracy. Colonel Thomas Hutchinson was one the richest merchants in

Boston. He owned a large mansion in the fashionable North End, an immense, three-story brick structure with two massive chimneys at each end. Inside, the richly furnished house was decorated with tapestries, sculptures, and oil paintings. There were extensive, beautiful gardens at the rear.

But it is Colonel Hutchinson's son, Thomas Jr., who played an important role in the story of Samuel Adams' life. In later years, as governor of Massachusetts Bay, he was destined to become one of Sam's bitterest enemies.

Thomas Jr. had everything that any young man could ask for. More than one Boston maiden sighed when she saw him, for he was handsome, tall and slender, with blue eyes and a fair complexion. He was rich and would be even richer when he inherited the colonel's great fortune. And like his father, he was a Boston selectman as well as a member of the House of Representatives of the Massachusetts Bay General Court.

But wealthy as he was, "Stingy Tommy," as some people called him, was greedy for more money, and willing to use almost any means to get it. He stood for all that Captain Adams did not. And since the English trade laws did not affect his livelihood, he did not object to the restrictions England placed upon the colonies.

Sam calmly accepted the news that his father was a ruined man. "I'll leave college," he said. "I'll go right to work."

"No," Captain Adams replied, "I want you to get your master's degree, Samuel."

Despite his son's protests, he remained firm. "The Land Bank's creditors will have to sue me in court in order to take my land," he said. "At least until that is decided, I will have the brewery. You will have to live economically, but you must finish your education."

Back to Harvard Sam went, his way of life greatly changed. He no longer dined outside the Yard. Instead, he got a job as a waiter in the Commons, serving the riotous students while getting his own meals free. And although he had never squandered the money his father had given him, he now had to make every penny do the work of a shilling. Not that Sam minded. In all his life he never cared much for the comforts money could buy. But there was a principle involved in the collapse of the Land Bank. He thought about that a great deal.

The English Parliament had put the Land Bank out of business after Governor Belcher, egged on by the Hutchinsons and other influential merchants, had tried but failed. The General Court would have had to pass a law suspending the bank's operations, and Sam knew that the governor would have had a hard time putting such a bill through. Bad as the Land Bank plan was, too many farmers, little merchants, artisans, and certain other people had been in favor of it.

Parliament made laws for the people of England, which was all right. If the people did not like the laws, they could elect new members of Parliament. But when the English government passed a law affecting Massachusetts Bay, the people of the colony could do nothing about it because they had no representatives in Parliament. That, to Sam Adams, did not seem right.

Among all the things he had learned about politics and government through his studies and by talking with his father, the tutors at Harvard, and his fellow students, two principles stood out most clearly in his mind. The first was that freedom-loving people had more than once asserted their independence by rising against a ruler who took away their rights; the second was that people who do not have a voice in the making of the laws that govern them are not truly free.

As time went on and Sam's second Commencement approached, these principles were uppermost in his mind as he prepared to write his thesis. This important paper would determine whether a candidate was qualified for his master's degree. And, as befitted such a proof of scholarship and learning, it would be written and declaimed in Latin.

Master's degrees were conferred upon the candidates in the afternoon, following the morning graduation of the senior sophister class and the great Commencement dinner.

That July day in 1743 was hot and sultry. In the breathless air of the Cambridge meetinghouse, on a platform erected at the front of the church, the dignitaries sat, glassy-eyed and stuffed with food. No doubt all of them wished heartily that this final ceremony was over. They knew that they were going to have to sit there until the last candidate for a master's degree had finished declaiming his thesis in an ancient language that most of them had all but forgotten since their college days. It would be very dull.

In the pulpit sat President Holyoke, wearing his academic gown. Before him, in a great chair at the front of the platform, was His Excellency, William Shirley, the new governor of Massachusetts Bay.

In the minds of many people the collapse of the Land Bank had had one good result at least; they had gotten rid of Governor Belcher. He had long been unpopular, and complaints about him had been sent to London earlier. More had followed when Belcher opposed the bank, and at last King George II, remembering how the people had risen against Sir Edmund Andros, had recalled him.

Seated on the platform, Governor Shirley was a fine-looking man in his powdered wig and his scarlet coat with its gold lace and white ruffles at the wrists and throat. He was different from his predecessor—aristocratic, yes, but not such a snob as Belcher had tended to be. With his commanding figure, firm mouth, and grave, discerning eyes, William Shirley carried the office of governor very well indeed.

Boston had long known him, for he had served there twelve years, first as a judge and then as advocate general of the Admiralty Court, which decided cases involving ships and sea trade.

"He's ambitious," people said of the new governor, "but he's able and he's honest. Maybe he can solve our money troubles."

After all the officials had assembled, President Holyoke arose and announced, *"Expectatur oratorio,"* signifying that the orations were about to begin. The first of the candidates advanced to the lectern and droned out the sonorous Latin phrases of his thesis. When he had finished, there was a polite patter of applause, although no one had really paid much attention. Some of the dignitaries were nodding. Even Governor Shirley looked drowsy.

The orations went on and on endlessly. But suddenly the governor roused with a start from his lethargy and sat upright, as did others on the platform. President Holyoke had just announced the subject of another thesis:

"An supremo Magistratui resistere liceat, si alter servasi Republica nequit. Affirmat respondens Samuel Adams."

Governor Shirley knew his Latin and was surprised at the title of the thesis: "Whether it be lawful to resist the Supreme Magistrate if the Commonwealth cannot otherwise be preserved. An affirmative view of the question by Samuel Adams."

Shirley directed his astonished gaze at President Holyoke. "What is this?" the look seemed to say. "Is a student at Harvard College to be permitted to argue in favor of rebellion against the King?"

Mr. Holyoke's calm expression did not change, however. He was a liberal, a college president who believed in letting his students do their own thinking and express their own ideas.

Governor Shirley then turned his scrutiny upon Samuel Adams, who was advancing toward the platform. Who was this young man? Adams. . . Samuel

Adams. He must be the son of Captain Adams, the Land Bank director. . . .

The governor knew Captain Adams. He knew about the Caulkers Club, too, made up of shipyard workers, rough fellows, the kind who had formed the mob that had seized Andros. As for young Adams and his thesis, it might not be treason, but it smelled of it.

The revolt against Andros had been bad enough, but to assert that rebellion against the King was justified. . . .

Governor Shirley was no tyrant like Andros. He sincerely wanted to get along with the people of Massachusetts Bay, to remedy their financial troubles and make life better for them. But he had been born in England and was a loyal subject of George II. He had been appointed governor by his sovereign and had sworn to uphold the Crown; yet here was Samuel Adams advocating revolt against the King if all else failed.

This young man would bear watching. . . .

～ Chapter 4 ～

For all his family's financial troubles, Samuel Adams faced the future in 1743 confidently. The world was his to conquer, as it is for any young man just out of college.

And Boston was a busy place. Big, too, as towns went in the American colonies. Seventeen thousand people lived there. Its many houses and shops were packed close together; the steeples of a round dozen of churches pointed the way to heaven.

In the heart of town, where King Street turned off from Cornhill and ran straight down to the harbor, the melee was something to stare at if you were a pumpkinhead in from the country on a visit. The cobblestone street was choked with carts, drays, and chaises, and the traffic overflowed onto the footways built for pedestrians on each side. But that hardly mattered, for everyone walked in the middle of the street anyway. Merchants, artisans, tradesmen, apprentices scattered like gabbling poultry before the horses' hoofs and the shouts and curses of the drivers.

The many other streets, most of them narrow, crooked lanes and alleys, had quaint names like Milk,

Fish, Ship, Moon, Sun, Seven Star, Crab, Frog, Mackerel, Flounder, Whitebread, and Turnagain. Near the center of town they were lined with the shops of wheelwrights, tallow chandlers, butchers, blacksmiths, silversmiths, wigmakers, upholsterers, barbers, printers, tanners, grocers, and booksellers. The shop signs showed what business was being conducted within, the Six Sugar Loaves, Three Horseshoes, Bible and Heart, Bull's Horns. And one shop where cloth was dyed showed a dog painted blue under an arching rainbow.

The quaintly named taverns, great and small, displayed their signs, too, the Bunch of Grapes, Green Dragon, Orange Tree, Dog and Pot, Half Moon, Black Horse, Lamb, Dove. In any one of these the weary traveler could find comfort and cheer. In summer the cool, dim interior offered him a pleasant respite from the heat. In winter he could toast his frostbitten feet before a crackling blaze in a cavernous fireplace. Supper was on the table. The wayfarer might choose from a roast of beef or ham or mutton, a fowl, a brace of lobsters, a haunch of venison, with a suet or boiled Indian pudding and a list of vegetables as long as his day's journey. These he could top off with a great slab of mince or pumpkin pie. Later it was good to relax and hear the news of the town from the apple-cheeked tavernkeeper and the citizens who gathered there, the smoke of their pipes curling upward toward the great hand-hewn summer beam of the taproom overhead. Afterward a snug bed awaited him.

Yes, Boston was a fine town, as Samuel Adams well knew. But the question was, what should he do?

He had given up the idea of becoming a lawyer. It is said that his mother objected to it, although there would seem to be no reason why she should. But since Sam would have had to be apprenticed to a lawyer in order to learn the profession, it seems more likely that he could not bear the thought of sitting in a dingy office, doing odd jobs and poking his nose into musty law books in between times.

"Tom Cushing needs a clerk in his countinghouse, Samuel," his father told him. "Now there's a good opportunity. He's not one of the biggest merchants, but he's doing well."

Merchant. . . it sounded interesting. Most merchants owned ships. Perhaps Sam remembered how ships had fascinated him in his boyhood days. "I'll go to see Mr. Cushing," he declared.

So off he went to the countinghouse hard by the waterfront, near the Town Dock, and was hired.

The job turned out to be extremely dull. All day long Sam sat perched like a dunce on a high stool with an enormous ledger open before him. For hours his quill pen and those of the other clerks scratched on and on. The slow tick-tock of a tall grandfather's clock in one corner, measuring the interminable hours, grated on his nerves. Outside, he could hear the muffled rattle of blocks and tackles and the creak of cordage. By looking up he could see the masts and spars of ships at the nearby wharves, but they were on the other side of the diamond-shaped window panes and might as well have been in China. Only when the captain of a tall frigate or brigantine swept in, bringing with him a smell of tar, a voice like the blast of a typhoon, and an air of adventure, did things liven up a bit.

As for the ciphering, as arithmetic was called, that was the worst of all. A ship's cargo sold abroad was often paid for in Spanish or Portuguese money, which circulated everywhere—reals, the piasters which were known as pieces of eight, pistoles, moidores, johannes. The values of these foreign coins had to be converted into English pounds, shillings, and pence and entered in the ledgers. The constant figuring made Sam's head ache. Money. . . sometimes he almost hated it.

All too often, on his way to work in the morning, or at midday when he returned from dinner, Sam would meet an acquaintance who, like himself, was interested in politics. They would strike up a conversation and loiter along, forgetting all about the passing of time.

Finally Mr. Cushing called Sam into his office. "I had great hopes for you, Samuel, when you came here to work," the old gentleman said, "but I have been somewhat disappointed. You are frequently late for work in the morning, or half the afternoon passes before you return. I hope you will take this warning in good spirit, my boy, for your father and I are old friends and I should regret having to dismiss you."

Sam looked down at the toes of his boots. "I shall try to do better, sir," he promised.

He did try, but somehow it did not work. He hated the countinghouse more than ever. Whenever he ran into someone to whom he could talk, Sam felt like a condemned man reprieved from the gallows. At last he was summoned to Mr. Cushing's office again.

The merchant shook his head sadly. "I am sorry but your tardiness forces me to discharge you, my boy. It is not that you are an idler by nature, for both your mind and your body are active. But you will never make a merchant; you are too wrapped up in politics. Please believe, Samuel, that I wish you well in whatever you undertake in the future."

"You are right, sir, I will never make a merchant." And more glad than sorry, Sam went home. The only thing he felt he had gained in the few months at the countinghouse was that he had met and become good friends with Mr. Cushing's son, Thomas Jr. Sam was destined to work side by side with the younger Cushing in the years preceding the Revolution.

"Perhaps you would do better to come into business with me," Captain Adams suggested. "The brewery is doing well and in time it will be yours."

"All right, Father," Sam replied. "I think I might like that."

He was not particularly interested in brewing beer and ale, but it offered him a living, and his father would not discharge him if he devoted some of his time to his real interest, politics. Captain Adams was beginning to prosper again. He was hopeful that the affairs of the Land Bank could be settled so that he would not lose his property.

Within a year or two, something happened that brought great prosperity to Massachusetts Bay. Governor Shirley had been determined to put the colony on a sound financial basis, and in 1745 his opportunity came. A new war had broken out in Europe. This meant that in Canada the French would be preparing to attack the New England settlements again. Governor Shirley decided to strike first, and boldly. He raised an army, collected a squadron of warships and transports, and sent both against the mighty French stronghold of Louisbourg at the tip end of Nova Scotia.

Few believed that it could be captured. William Pepperrell, commander of the army, was not a military man but a merchant, his soldiers untrained farmers and fishermen. But they besieged Louisbourg, gave it a terrible pounding with their cannon, and forced its surrender.

There was a wild celebration when the news reached Boston, but to Shirley the victory meant more than an occasion for ringing church bells and setting off fireworks. He sent his son-in-law to London to demand that Massachusetts Bay be repaid for its contribution toward winning the war.

The King and his ministers decided that the claim was a just one, and some months later a ship arrived in Boston and moored at the immense Long Wharf that jutted out two thousand feet into the harbor at the foot of King Street. The people stared openmouthed as twenty-seven huge wagons lumbered up King Street toward the colony's treasury. Each was loaded with money chests of shining silver pieces of eight and casks of copper coin worth nearly two hundred thousand pounds.

Shirley found ways and means to keep the vast sum from flowing back to England. Massachusetts Bay's envious neighbor provinces to the south began to call her "the hard-money colony." And the businessmen of Boston prospered, the Adamses, father and son, along with them.

Being associated with his father in the malthouse on Purchase Street was not what Sam really wanted, but he was happy enough. He found time to organize a political club of his own with some of his friends.

The club's activities were secret, but the members started a newspaper called the *Independent Advertiser*. In it they printed articles about liberty and people's rights. Sam wrote more than anyone else. They continually criticized Governor Shirley, who did not actually deserve it, and other members of the colony's royal government.

No one knew the club's name, but people said, "They ought to call it the Whipping Post Club. They're always chastising somebody in that newspaper of theirs."

It was about this time that Sam Adams suffered a great loss. At the age of fifty-seven his father died. The cause of his death is not known, but it came as a severe blow to Sam. Captain Adams had been the kindest and most indulgent of fathers. Sam did not realize until some years later how acutely the loss of his father was to affect his welfare.

Sam continued to operate the brewery although not too successfully. Between that, the political club, and his writings for the *Independent Advertiser*, he kept so busy that he had little time to dwell upon his grief. And then Betty Checkley came into his life.

Sam had been baptized by the Reverend Samuel Checkley. When the Adamses attended church services on the Sabbath, Sam could look over at the minister's pew and see his pretty daughter. He liked what he saw very much. Betty, probably perfectly well aware of his glances, kept her eyes modestly lowered and tried not to blush.

So Sam went "sparking" Betty Checkley. For a time his courting was a very stiff and formal affair. From what is known of courtship in colonial days, it is easy to visualize him calling upon her at the parsonage, dressed in his best suit of homespun and looking to his manners. Sam was no "macaroni," as dandies were called then, but Mrs. Adams no doubt saw to it that there were no spots on her son's coat and breeches, that his shoes were well brushed and his wig tidy.

Since he first had to ask permission to call, the entire Checkley family was ready for him, except for the younger children who had been put to bed earlier. Everyone was seated primly in the parlor, a room with a cold and forbidding air which ordinarily was used only for weddings, funerals, and other important occasions. Sam's eyes fell upon Betty, seated demurely in a distant corner, intent upon the sampler she was working, but he greeted her father and mother first. Then he selected a chair in the corner farthest from the object of his affections.

Mrs. Checkley asked after Sam's mother, sister, and younger brother Joseph. Then followed a discussion of Mr. Checkley's sermon the previous Sabbath and of the weather. Those subjects having been dis-

43

posed of, there was an agonizing silence while Sam desperately cast about for something else to say. Now and then he dared to steal a quick glance in Betty's direction. He thought she looked lovely in her best gown of blue calico, with her hair sleek and glossy under a fresh white mob cap. Only once did she meet his gaze, and the mischievous look in her eyes made him wonder if she was laughing at him.

He was relieved when the tall clock in the hallway struck nine and Mr. Checkley coughed loudly. That was Sam's cue to depart, for people went to bed early in Boston. Sam rose and took his leave, bidding Betty good night last of all. They had not exchanged two words the whole evening, but once again she gave him a look from under her lashes and he felt better, for her eyes said, "Come back, Sam."

After several such visits Sam was permitted to sit closer to her and use a courting stick. This was a hollow wooden tube, an inch in diameter and six or eight feet long, through which he and Betty could whisper to each other while their elders, more at ease now, carried on their own conversations.

Finally, when the Checkleys were sure that the young man's intentions were serious, Mr. Checkley would say when the clock struck nine, "Bedtime, Mother. We'll leave the young folks by themselves." And upstairs they would go, having blown out the candles, leaving only a tiny light known as a sparking lamp.

And so Betty and Sam were married on October 17, 1749, by her father, and took up their married life in the house on Purchase Street.

There is no record to show whether Sam's mother lived with them. Nor do we know how long she lived, though she was alive when Captain Adams died, since his will left her part of his estate. In the Adams family Bible, Captain Adams and later Sam kept records of births, deaths, and marriages, but there is no mention of Mrs. Adams' death. So it seems probable that she either married again or went to live with her daughter Mary, who was now Mrs. Joseph Allen, and lived in one of the towns outside Boston.

Sam's financial troubles grew steadily worse. The brewery, which had earned Captain Adams a substantial fortune, no longer prospered under the son's management. Competitors took advantage of the fact that Sam was no businessman, and his income steadily decreased. It was then he realized that his father's death meant more than the loss of a loving parent and friend.

Through it all, Betty Adams' love and faith in him never wavered. She was convinced that someday her husband would be a very great man. She found ways to economize and make do with little money; nevertheless the house on Purchase Street began to look run down. More and more, needed repairs had to be put off because Sam could not afford them.

Sam's appearance must have been his wife's despair. He simply could not keep himself tidy. He had few clothes, and those he owned were shabby and full of spots and stains. Betty Adams did her best to keep them clean and neat but it was a hopeless effort. He always wore the same red cloak, which became the trade-mark by which all of Boston knew him. There was a slight stoop to his walk, and his hair began to turn gray at an early age, which made him look much older than he was. Despite his appearance, his courtesy and gentle manners made him well liked by the poor and the wealthy alike.

Five children were born to the Adamses, but only two of them, Samuel Jr. and Hannah, lived beyond infancy. Although babies are tough little creatures, many were not able to withstand either the long, bitter winters in houses heated only by fireplaces or the diseases for which doctors then knew no cure.

In 1757 Governor Shirley's efficient administration came to an end when he was recalled to England and Thomas Pownall appointed in his place. Bostonians liked the new governor, who upheld and respected the rights of the American colonies. That may explain the fact that Pownall and Sam Adams became good friends.

Meanwhile Sam continued to write articles for the *Independent Advertiser* and other Boston newspapers, warning the citizens that the time was not far distant when England would try to control her colonies more strictly. People had better look to their rights, he cautioned. But Massachusetts Bay was prospering and no one paid much attention. Nevertheless Sam kept on writing.

Another and more terrible blow than the loss of his father lay just ahead. On July 5, 1757, Elizabeth Adams died after giving birth to a dead baby. Stricken by grief, beset by money troubles, and left with two small children to bring up, Sam scarcely knew which way to turn.

Indeed, the months that followed were dark ones. It had been seventeen years since the Land Bank had gone out of business; yet its creditors still had not been paid in full for their losses. At breakfast one morning in August, 1758, Sam was reading the weekly edition of the Boston *News-Letter*. His startled eye fell on a notice signed by the sheriff:

To be sold at public Auction, at the Exchange Tavern in Boston. Tomorrow at noon, the Dwelling House, Malt-House, and other buildings, with the Garden and lands adjoining, and the Wharf, Dock and Flats before the same, being part of the estate of the late Samuel Adams, Esq., deceased . . . the said estate being taken by warrant or execution with the hand and seal of the Hon. Commissioners for the more speedy finishing of the Land Bank scheme.

Sam was aghast. He and his children would be homeless, his business, such as it was, lost completely. He rose, went to his writing table, took a sheet of paper, dipped his quill, and composed a terse letter to the sheriff:

"Sir, I observe your advertisement for the sale of the Estate of Samuel Adams, Esq., director of the Land Bank Company," he wrote. He stated his belief that the sale was illegal and then added, "I am determined to prosecute to the law any person whomsoever who shall trespass upon that Estate."

Perhaps the sheriff feared that if he came to sell the property Sam might greet him with a loaded musket. Whatever his reason, he postponed the auction for a month. Then put it off another week. The sale was never held, so Sam kept his home, the malthouse, and the land.

Not that owning the brewery did him much good. Business had dwindled to almost nothing. The building itself was beginning to fall apart, and the house was not in much better condition.

Even though some of Sam's friends had come to his aid, their efforts had brought a new trouble. Sorry to see him growing shabbier, some of the Boston selectmen had discussed his plight in 1756.

"Sam doesn't seem to make a go of anything," one had remarked, "but he's a fine, intelligent fellow. Honest, too. Can't we find a job for him?"

"Why not make him tax collector?" someone else suggested.

"The very thing," they all agreed. The pay was reasonably good. It would enable Sam Adams to keep a roof, tumble-down as it was, over his family's head. At the town meeting that year he had been nominated for the job of tax collector, and since everyone had great affection for him, he was elected easily.

Now, however, because his own money troubles made him sympathetic to others who had them, he was in difficulties. As he made his rounds, calling upon those who had not paid their taxes, the delinquents would say, "I'm having trouble collecting my own bills, Sam. But I expect some money next week—can you let my taxes go until then?"

And Sam, generous and kind hearted, would nod his head. "I understand."

48

Unfortunately, in many cases, "next week" never came. The amount of uncollected taxes increased steadily in the years that followed. At last, when the town meeting was held in 1764, Sam stood before the people with his head bowed. "I have served you badly," he said. "Nearly seven thousand pounds of unpaid taxes remain uncollected. I appreciate the honor you have done me, but I must decline to serve for another year."

He had done badly, true, but the people would have none of that kind of talk; they liked him too well. He was voted back into office for another year.

Samuel Adams was nearly forty-two years old and had never succeeded at anything. He had lost his wife, the business his father had left him was gone, and his house was falling down about his ears. He was a failure.

But at this lowest ebb of his life, better times lay just ahead. Not better financially, but he would soon find new happiness in his home and new inspiration in a series of events that would bring him to the fore as a great American patriot. The tiny spark of independence he had lighted was about to flare up and burn with a hotter flame.

Chapter 5

FOR SEVERAL YEARS England had had a new King, and now Massachusetts Bay again had a new governor.

The King was George III, a sober, dignified young man. Perhaps the worst thing that could be said about him was that he was obstinate. And he liked working in his gardens better than ruling England and presiding over all the boring official functions that he was obliged to attend. For that reason the people of England called him "Farmer George."

In Boston the new governor was Francis Bernard. The colonists were sorry to see Thomas Pownall leave, but they hoped they would like Bernard as much. He was given an enthusiastic welcome, but all too soon trouble began. At least part of the reason was the fact that Boston was prospering. Only a few years earlier, Beacon Hill, which loomed over the town, had been pasture land; on its summit stood a tall beacon pole with a barrel of tar at its top, to be lighted as an alarm in case of an attack. But now wealthy citizens were building elegant mansions up there as well as in other parts of the town.

It was no longer enough to build a house of plain timbers, which in time weathered to a pretty silver-gray. It had to be painted, or better still, built of English brick. The wives of prosperous men in Boston no longer spun and wove flax and wool into homespun and made their clothes of it. They insisted on having the latest modes in silks and satins from London to wear to church, to teas, to balls. Now more and more ships departed for Massachusetts Bay loaded with fine cloth, gowns, laces, and other fripperies as well as bricks, paint, and varnish. Crown officials returning to London declared that people in Boston lived almost as well as English lords and ladies and put on just as many airs.

It caused some talk in England, and no doubt some resentment. "America is getting rich," certain noblemen and high government officials complained. "What good does that do England? The colonies are ours; yet they don't pay the Crown a penny of taxes."

"That's not the worst of it," returning travelers would add. "The merchants are getting rich by breaking the King's laws. Everyone in Boston knows that half the goods that arrive are smuggled in."

It was true. The laws that forbade the colonies to buy anything but English goods were winked at. Ships came into Boston from Holland, from France, from the French islands of the West Indies and unloaded their cargoes secretly.

"This must stop," Parliament finally announced, and reinforced the trade laws by permitting customs officials, armed only with documents called "writs of assistance," to enter not only colonial warehouses but also people's homes to search for smuggled goods. It was a foolish thing to do. The enraged people of Boston directed their indignation at Governor Bernard and the younger Thomas Hutchinson, who upheld the new law. Perhaps there was not much else they could have done. As officials of the royal government they had sworn to serve their King loyally. But that fact did not prevent a storm of indignation from sweeping down on both of them.

Old Thomas Hutchinson had died, and his son had inherited his fortune and great mansion. Thomas Jr. was now a very important man in the government of Massachusetts Bay. He was not only the colony's lieutenant governor but its chief justice, a judge of probate, and a member of the governor's Council. It was particularly infuriating to the people that a man who had been born in Boston should support the writs of assistance.

Samuel Adams might not have had the ability to make money, but when it came to politics there was no smarter man in Boston. In the trouble over the writs he saw his chance to arouse the people against British injustice. And now he had the help of two strong men.

One was his second cousin, John Adams, a lawyer who lived in the village of Braintree, outside Boston. He was thirteen years younger than Sam and of very different temperament, yet the two were fast friends and were to work side by side in the struggle for liberty. John always called Sam "my brother Adams." The other man was the friend of Sam's Harvard College days, fiery James Otis. Although twenty years had passed, time had done nothing to calm Otis down. John Adams called this lawyer and rampaging orator "a flame of fire."

A suit was begun to challenge the legality of the writs. John Adams and James Otis were among the lawyers for the opposition. Otis made an impassioned speech, striding up and down the courtroom and looking for all the world like a bull about to charge at the dignified judges in their crimson robes and great wigs. "A man is as secure in his house as a prince in his castle!" he thundered. And he was right. For many years it had been a principle of English law that "a man's house is his castle" and that no one could enter it without permission.

Samuel Adams was no orator. He spoke well, but he was handicapped by the palsy that made his voice as well as his hands tremble. His most powerful weapon was his pen, as Bostonians well knew from reading his articles and letters in the newspapers. Often, during the noon hours, he strolled down to the shipyards, perched on one of the short posts called bollards, which were used to secure ships' mooring lines, and talked to the workmen as they ate their dinners. He did not use Otis' fiery oratory and gestures, but his audience listened just as intently.

Meanwhile Sam was seeing a good deal of an old friend of his father. Francis Wells had been a merchant in England before coming to America and settling in Boston. One of his five daughters, Elizabeth, was at that time twenty-four years old. It was Betsy, as Sam called her, whom he particularly came to see when he called on the Wells family.

Betsy Wells was a lovely young woman and as good as she was pretty. Sam and Betsy fell in love, and they were married on December 6, 1764. She must indeed have been deeply in love to marry shabby, impecunious Samuel Adams, now 42, and go to live in the old house in Purchase Street that was more rickety and tumble-down than ever. And along with Sam, she had to take his two children. Sam Jr. was thirteen and Hannah eight, both of them at ages where they needed a mother badly.

Samuel Adams was unfortunate in many things during his life, but not in his two marriages. Betsy Adams made the best of poverty and the old house, gave the children love and care, and did what she could to keep her husband looking presentable. Not that the cleverest wife in the world could have made a dandy of him. "If I sew a button on Sam's sleeve in the morning, it is always off before nightfall," Betsy once said wryly.

In that year, 1764, Samuel Adams put an important idea into words for the first time. "If taxes are laid upon us in any shape without our having a legal representative where they are laid," he wrote, "are we not reduced from the character of subjects to the miserable state of tributary slaves?"

Later on, that same idea would be expressed in the battle cry of other American patriots: "No taxation without representation!"

Eventually the furor over the writs of assistance

died down. James Otis and John Adams were unsuccessful in having them declared illegal, but after the suit they were not used as frequently. From then on, until the outbreak of the Revolution, no sooner had one quarrel between the colonies and England been smoothed over than another action on the part of the British government started trouble again.

In 1765 the trouble was much more serious. This time the lawmakers in England, in need of additional revenue for the Crown, passed the Stamp Act, placing a direct tax on all colonial publications and legal documents. There was immediate consternation and alarm, not only in Boston but throughout the American colonies. Lawyers were especially hard hit, but everybody protested the fact that all wills, deeds, ships' clearance papers, newspapers, even marriage certificates, had to be stamped. A college diploma was worthless unless it had a government stamp on it that cost two pounds, about $5.60 in our money today. True, the stamp for a newspaper cost only a halfpenny, but every stamp was a *tax*.

Samuel Adams's quill pen fairly flew over the paper now. It was well known in Boston that he was the author of the many letters that appeared in the newspapers defending the people's rights. Instead of signing his own name he used "A Puritan," "A Bostonian," "Candidus," "Vindex," and other pseudonyms, but this fooled no one. Just by the subject matter and the style everyone knew perfectly well that the letters were Sam's work.

Not only did Sam have the help of Otis and his

cousin now, but America had a few friends in London, too. Some of the government leaders were not in favor of taxing the colonies. Along with the details of the Stamp Act, another piece of news reached Boston; Colonel Isaac Barré, a member of Parliament, had defended the colonies' rights in a violent debate before the Stamp Act was passed.

"The people," he had cried, "I believe are as truly loyal as any subjects the King has, but a people jealous of their liberties, and who will vindicate them if ever they should be violated." He had called the people of America "those sons of liberty."

One night not long afterward a meeting was held in Boston, so secret that even the meeting place is not known. Most of those present were working men—mechanics, shipyard workers, and the like—as well as some of the patriot leaders. It seems certain that Samuel Adams was present, for that night a society was organized to defend the rights of the people against the Crown, and he became one of its leading figures.

"What shall we call ourselves?" someone asked during the meeting.

Someone else—and it may well have been Sam Adams, for he always had an ear for a good phrase or slogan—replied, "Colonel Barré described us very well when he called us the Sons of Liberty. I suggest we adopt that name!"

They all cheered. And that was the way the Sons of Liberty, which was to spread throughout all the American colonies, began.

The group kept its activities as well as the names

of its members secret. In the years between 1765 and the beginning of the Revolution in 1775, a number of disturbances took place in Boston, and each time the word got around that the Sons of Liberty were behind it. No one could prove that Samuel Adams was actually involved in such affairs. Nevertheless, throughout the pre-Revolutionary period, he exercised control over events which led the American colonies toward war in much the same manner that the little figures in a puppet show are manipulated by the puppeteer. Adams stayed behind the scenes and pulled the strings. By writing and talking, he was able to influence public opinion against injustice and infringement of the people's rights as Englishmen. But he let them do the acting. In the riots and demonstrations that took place between 1765 and 1775, he was rarely seen. But he was there, behind the curtain.

The Stamp Act was not to go into effect until November, but long before that things began to happen. Who or what caused them is not known. We know only that Samuel Adams' pen and tongue were very busy and that the leaders of the Sons of Liberty continued to hold secret meetings.

Andrew Oliver, secretary of the royal government of Massachusetts Bay, was appointed stamp master to handle the distribution of stamps. He was a rich man who lived in a big mansion in the South End of Boston, not far from Samuel Adams. He kept a coach, a chariot, and fine horses in his stables; his house was luxuriously furnished and hung with oil paintings; his table was set with the heaviest sterling silver. His appointment alone, not to mention that he was a brother-in-law of Lieutenant Governor Thomas Hutchinson, was enough to stir the people's anger against him. If Oliver had known what he was getting into, he probably would never have accepted the job.

At dawn on August 14, 1765, early risers in Boston—workingmen going to their jobs and housewives making an early start for market to get the best selection of meats and vegetables—stopped in Hanover Square, their mouths agape, to stare at the giant elm that people had begun to refer to as the Liberty Tree. From one of its branches hung a dummy stuffed with straw and wearing a pair of yellow breeches. A noose was drawn tight about its neck. No one had any trouble recognizing the person it was meant to represent. Whoever had made it had caught perfectly the long-nosed, aristocratic expression of Andrew Oliver.

Beside the effigy hung a huge boot with a figure of the devil, horns and all, peeping out over the top. No one had any trouble understanding what that meant either. The boot signified Lord Bute, a close adviser of the King and one of the most hated men in England, who had been instrumental in securing the passage of the Stamp Act.

The dummies were comical; yet no one laughed. That was the ominous thing about it. They hung there all day, and no one made any attempt to take them down. Passers-by simply stopped, stared, and went on. But that evening at dusk a crowd began to collect at the Liberty Tree, gathering quickly, as though some sort of signal had been given. By the time someone stepped forward and cut down the dummy of Andrew Oliver, two thousand people were there.

Then, once more as if signaled, the crowd moved off, with two men in the lead carrying the effigy of Oliver. The mob surged toward the Town House at the head of King Street, where Governor Bernard and his Council, including Oliver and Lieutenant Governor Hutchinson, were meeting.

The people marched straight through the building without stopping. Someone started a measured chant that swelled to a roar from two thousand throats, setting a cadence for the tramping feet: "Liberty . . . property . . . no stamps!"

Then the mob headed down King Street. At the waterfront, where it ended, Andrew Oliver had a wharf. On it stood a small new building believed to be the office where the stamps would be distributed.

"Break it down!" an angry voice shouted. A furious clunking of broadaxes swung by brawny mechanics and shipyard men began. Timbers shrieked protestingly as the axes ripped and splintered them. In five minutes there was nothing left of the building but a pile of smashed-up kindling.

A cry went up: "To Fort Hill!" With a wild yell of triumph the mob surged forth again. As the uncontrollable rioters passed Oliver's house, they stormed it, breaking windows, smashing furniture, and drinking all the wine in the cellar while the stamp master's terrified family crouched behind barricaded doors in their bedchambers. Finally the mob moved on to Fort Hill by the harbor, lit a huge bonfire with the shattered timbers of the stamp office, then beheaded and burned Andrew Oliver's effigy.

But that was not the end of the rioting. For almost two weeks the leaders of the disturbance lay low. Then, on August 26, when things had apparently quieted down, the mob gathered again.

After a blistering hot day in Boston, the evening was breathless. In the immense brick mansion in fashionable North Square Lieutenant Governor Thomas Hutchinson and his family were trying to keep cool. His wife had died some years before, but his three sons and two daughters were with him.

Suddenly there came a furious hammering at the front door. When Hutchinson hurriedly threw it open, one of his friends burst in, panting hard. "The mob's out!" he exclaimed. "They're talking about pulling down your house, Tom. You'd all better get out of here!"

"No," said Hutchinson, "I'll stay and face them."

"Elisha and I will stay with you, Father," said Thomas, the elder of the two grown sons.

"Good," replied the lieutenant governor. He turned to his sister-in-law, who was standing nearby with his younger children. "Grizzel, take the two younger ones to the neighbor's." To his oldest daughter he added, "Go with them, Sallie."

Although the young girl pleaded to be allowed to stay, her father refused. But just as Hutchinson and the two older boys were barricading the door with heavy furniture, Sallie returned, having escaped her aunt.

Hysterical with terror, she sobbed, "If you're going to die, I'm going to die with you, Father!"

For a moment Hutchinson did not reply. His ear caught the first ominous sound of the approaching mob. He could not know that the men had already burst into the houses of a judge and a customs commissioner on the way and had drunk all the wine in their cellars. But he could tell from the sound that they were ugly and dangerous.

He could not leave Sallie there to face them, so he took her with him to the neighbor's house. His two sons stayed until the mob battered in the front door. Then they fled to safety through the rear.

The rioters burst in. They swarmed over the house from top to bottom, smashing everything they could lay their hands on, hurling the broken and tattered remains of furniture, paintings, hangings, clocks, china, and clothing through the shattered windows. They stole money, silverware, and jewelry. They drank the wine cellar dry. When there was nothing left to break or steal, they tore out the paneling on the walls. Some of the men got up on the roof and pried part of it off.

Soon nothing remained of the beautiful mansion but an empty shell. Then the rioters rushed to the lovely gardens in the rear. They trampled everything in them flat, tore down the garden house, and pulled up fruit trees by the roots.

What part did Samuel Adams play in this shameful raid upon the property of Thomas Hutchinson, who had kept his oath to the Crown by defending the King's laws? No one knows. True, he hated the lieutenant governor for more reasons than one, but he did not want to provoke the English into taking strong retaliatory measures. It was not yet the time for armed revolt, and Sam Adams knew it.

Nevertheless, he had stirred the people against the Crown by his writings and speeches, and he must share in the blame. Once the people were aroused, they had to release their anger somehow. Such rioting would occur more than once before the first musket roared on the village green at Lexington.

$\backsim$ Chapter 6 $\backsim$

AT A TOWN meeting before the Stamp Act went into effect, Samuel Adams was elected to the General Court to fill a vacancy created by the death of one of Boston's representatives. It was just like Sam, of course, to fall into a job that would require much of his time and pay no salary. But it was exactly what he wanted. Now, as a member of the House of Representatives, which made the colony's laws and acted as the people's spokesmen to the governor and the Crown, he could use his pen and voice to even greater advantage.

Sam began to work more closely with his friend James Otis who, as one of the four Boston representatives in the General Court, was very influential. Otis at the time was considered the leader of the Whig, or patriot, party. Another of Sam's fellow members was Tom Cushing, whom he had met years ago while working in the Cushings' countinghouse.

Otis saw to it that Sam was appointed to all the important committees of the House of Representatives. There was much writing for him to do, drafting laws, reports, and communications to the governor and the leaders of the British government in London. In fact, whatever Otis himself wrote he gave to Sam to read and "quieu whew," as he called it. Where he got such an odd expression no one knew, but he explained that it meant "to pour a little oil on them." He recognized Sam's talent for making letters, petitions, or resolutions more persuasive by a change here and there.

It was not long before the two were the most powerful members of the House. Between James Otis' fiery speechmaking and his way of dominating people and Samuel Adams' ability to win them over by writing or simply talking to them, they were able to influence other representatives and gain their support.

In October, James Otis and a group of other leaders went to New York, where delegates from nine of the American colonies met in what became known as the Stamp Act Congress. The congress petitioned the King and Parliament to repeal the Stamp Act. But it was too late, of course, to keep it from going into effect on November 1.

When that day dawned, church bells all over Boston tolled slowly and mournfully, the way they did when someone had died and they pealed the years of his age. Ships owned by Boston merchants flew their flags at half-mast. Dummies of British government leaders were hung from the Liberty Tree and then burned. But there was no rioting.

Instead, the people of Boston simply ignored the Stamp Act. Newspapers came out as usual, but there were no halfpenny stamps on them. Ships arrived in Boston and sailed away again without having their manifests, bills of lading, or clearance papers stamped.

Sam Adams must have been pleased to learn that all through the American colonies it was the same; no one would buy stamps. He had long ago realized that independence could never be won unless the colonies united against the Crown. He must have also been pleased when a new Boston newspaper, *The Constitutional Courant,* appeared, its front-page banner showing a snake divided into the same number of pieces as there were colonies, and the motto, JOIN OR DIE.

There was still no real violence, although the colonies did force their stamp masters to resign. In Boston, Andrew Oliver, who by this time was frightened out of his wits, was marched to the Liberty Tree and made to give up his job, which he did with the greatest relief.

The strongest blow of all against Governor Bernard was that the courts were closed, save for the higher ones administered by the Crown government. Without stamps on all the writs, warrants, and other documents they issued, they could not operate, and the officials of the lower courts refused to buy the stamps.

A committee that included Samuel Adams, John Adams, and James Otis was appointed to go before the governor and his Council and ask that the courts be allowed to reopen without using the stamps. Otis outdid himself in the speech he delivered on that occasion. He became so wrought up that tears rolled down his cheeks as he spoke. But the request was refused.

Nevertheless, Francis Bernard knew that something had to be done, and soon. He had been appointed to govern the province of Massachusetts Bay. If he failed, he would be recalled to England in disgrace. And without the courts he could not succeed. A Parliament or a Congress or a General Court can make laws, but only the courts of law can enforce them. If those in Massachusetts Bay did not reopen soon, there might as well be no government at all.

Doubtless Bernard's refusal did not displease Samuel Adams. This closing of the courts was a better weapon for him than all the riots and howling mobs in the world. And in England the cooler heads also knew it. The Stamp Act had been passed in Parliament by a very large majority; now many members who had voted for it began to fear that they had made a serious mistake. Fortunately for Governor Bernard, a powerful figure in the English government and a great friend of America, William Pitt, urged Parliament to repeal the Stamp Act. In March, 1766, it was repealed.

When the news reached Boston in May, there was a tremendous celebration. Every bell in town pealed wildly all day, and from the fort on Castle Island and all the ships in the harbor came the roar of saluting cannon. That evening the Liberty Tree blazed with lanterns hung in its branches. Beyond it, up on the Common, was a towering pyramid of oiled paper with three hundred lanterns glowing inside it.

On that balmy spring evening the narrow, crooked streets were jammed with people headed toward the Common. Shabby, lean-jawed ropewalk and shipyard workers in homespun coats and leather breeches hurried along with an expectant glimmer in their tired eyes. Teen-aged apprentices skylarked, whistling shrilly, chasing each other like squirrels, and bumping into dignified merchants and their families. Sailors in wide

66

petticoat breeches and varnished leather hats cast sheep's eyes at girls in bright calico dresses, who giggled and pretended not to see them.

From the Common the people could see Beacon Hill's broad back looming up darkly against the twilight sky. Up there, John Hancock's great mansion was brilliantly lighted.

As the immense crowd gazed at the spectacle of the illuminated pyramid, there were shouts of, "Make way, there!" The people fell back to let a wagon pulled by two horses rumble onto the Common. It was loaded with four big casks.

A man in servant's livery next to the driver stood up and raised his hand. "Mr. John Hancock's been pleased to send down some Madeira with his compliments," he announced. "Now, give us a hand here, some of you, with these pipes of wine."

Those nearest the wagon needed no second invitation. The ponderous casks were hoisted out in a trice and as quickly broached. Mr. Hancock's servant then produced a wicker basket heaped with pewter mugs. Filling one himself, he held it aloft.

"Come on, all of you, and pledge a loyal toast to His Majesty, our good King George!" he cried, and the crowd pressed forward.

Whether Samuel Adams was among those on the Common, we do not know. If not, he was one of the few people in Boston who did not get there. If he was present, however, he must have smiled wryly to himself as he watched John Hancock's gift being handed out and heard the crowd cheer.

Not long before, Sam and his cousin John had been strolling about Boston. They were so deep in a discussion of politics that they scarcely noticed where their footsteps were taking them. At length they found themselves at the foot of Beacon Hill.

Sam Adams had pointed toward the Hancock mansion. "I have done a very good thing for our cause by enlisting that young man into it," he observed to John, "and a wise thing by making his fortune ours."

He had spoken the truth. John Hancock was one of the richest men in Boston. From his uncle, Thomas Hancock, a merchant, he had inherited the magnificent house on Beacon Hill, a large fortune, and a prosperous business. Like many wealthy men in America, he had at first favored the Crown, until Sam Adams, with his persuasive talk, had gotten hold of him. When war came, the patriots were going to need John Hancock, and his fortune.

It was dark by the time the wine was consumed. Suddenly there was a *Pow*! and a rocket shot into the sky, bursting with a thunderous explosion into a shower of golden stars. The fireworks had begun. A series of skyrockets hurtled up to an admiring chorus of "Ohs!" and "Ahs!" There were also many set pieces, including a marvelous sparkling beehive with a swarm of golden bees streaming out of it. When at last the great celebration was over, everyone went home, happy and loyal once more to King George III.

Perhaps not quite everyone, however. . . . Samuel Adams could not have been pleased at the demonstration of revived good will toward England, but the shift in public opinion did not prevent him from continuing his agitation against the Crown. If he did not change people's feelings immediately, he at least kept the issues alive in their minds by his writings.

Meanwhile another of Boston's yearly town meetings was held. Samuel Adams was again elected to the House of Representatives of the General Court. James Otis and Tom Cushing were also re-elected, and there was a new representative from Boston, John Hancock. Perhaps some of Samuel Adams' friends in the House of Representatives decided to take pity on his poverty and shabbiness, for when it met soon after the great celebration, he was elected its clerk. That meant he would receive a small salary. It was only about one hundred pounds a year, but it was something, and while it probably meant very little to Sam, Betsy Adams was surely thankful for it.

More trouble with England was not long in coming. Charles Townshend, the Chancellor of the Exchequer, who handled financial matters for the Crown, was concerned about the four hundred thousand pounds it cost each year to maintain the colonies in America. An ambitious man, he hoped to further his political career by saving the government some of this money. Despite the fact that taxing the colonies had already resulted in storms of protest, Townshend proposed to place customs duties on a number of the goods the colonials imported in large quantities—glass, lead, paint, paper, and tea. Although his plan met with considerable opposition in Parliament, the large revenue it would bring in was too significant to be rejected. So, in 1767 the Townshend

Acts were passed. Determined to make the most of the opportunity, the chancellor also appointed royal Commissioners of Customs to replace the lax colonial officials who turned their heads the other way and allowed merchants to smuggle in contraband.

As was to be expected, the new act created another storm of outrage and objection. All the good will that England had regained by repealing the Stamp Act immediately vanished as patriot leaders everywhere in America stirred up anger and fear. The colonies had to retaliate in some way before the English government decided to impose more, and heavier, taxes.

"We can defeat the Townshend Act the same way we did the Stamp Act," said some leaders. "If the Crown is determined to tax us for the things we have to buy from England, we will stop buying them!"

Samuel Adams worked with furious energy. When the House of Representatives decided to send petitions against the Townshend Act to England, Sam drafted the letters that were to go to all the King's ministers, including William Pitt. One was addressed to the Lords of the Treasury; another was sent to King George himself.

The petitions were long and had to be written with great skill and exactness. Samuel Adams was so busy with his duties in the House of Representatives that he had to write the letters at home. Evening after evening, in the living room of the old house on Purchase Street, he sat working on them.

It is not hard to imagine the scene, the candlelit room with its furniture sadly dilapidated by long use;

Sam in his soiled old brown coat, his uncombed wig askew, sitting hunched over a writing table piled high with papers and documents, scratching away with his quill. A cheerful blaze crackled on the hearth, though not too large a one, for firewood was expensive.

In a chair drawn up to the fire Betsy Adams sat knitting, her placid face revealing nothing of all the problems she faced bravely each day. Nearby, Sam's daughter Hannah, now twelve, worked a sampler. Sam Jr. was not there, for in spite of poverty his father had managed to send him to Harvard so that he could become a doctor. Sprawled on the floor, Sam's immense Newfoundland dog Queue was dozing. People said, "Now, isn't that just like Sam Adams to have a dog so big it eats him out of house and home?"

On one such evening Hannah looked up from her needlework. "Who is it you are writing to now, Father?" she asked.

Sam's pen did not stop moving over the paper. "To the King," he murmured.

Hannah's eyes grew wide. "The King!" she breathed. "Just think! That paper you have in front of you will soon be touched by his royal hand!"

Laying down his quill, Sam turned toward his daughter. He was smiling in his grave way. "It will more likely be kicked by his royal foot, my dear," he said.

Samuel Adams' petitions were excellently written though his whole heart could scarcely have been in the task. His purposes were better suited if England continued to tax the colonies. Yet he labored hard on his task for in the back of his head an idea was simmering.

"Now that we have sent these petitions to England," he suggested to his fellow patriots, "why don't we write a circular letter to all the other colonies, telling them what we have done and asking them to do the same?"

There it was again, the idea that the colonies must be united against England.

The House of Representatives passed a resolution authorizing the sending of the circular letter. Samuel Adams was asked to write it, and a masterly job he did. An enthusiastic response was received from all the other colonies.

In England, however, the news of the letter was received with anger and concern. One rebellious colony was bad enough, but if they all got together. . . . Lord Hillsborough, Secretary of State for the Colonies, sent a stern, wrathful letter to the House of Representatives, commanding the members, in the name of the King, to repeal the resolution and to retract publicly everything that was written in the circular letter.

The representatives, by a vote of 92 to 17, refused. In a rage, Governor Bernard used his authority to end the session of the General Court and sent the representatives home. But he was sufficiently alarmed by the situation to send a request to London for British troops and a fleet of warships to preserve law and order in Boston.

The Sons of Liberty were still holding their secret meetings. Among their members were those who acted as spies, making it their business to know what went on in Boston's royal government circles. At that time the Sons of Liberty became especially interested in John Hancock's sloop, the "Liberty."

The "Liberty" had just returned from a voyage. When the customs officers, called tide-waiters, came aboard, the captain invited them into his cabin, where he poured out some wine for them.

"Taste this, boys," he told them. "I think you'll like it; it's the finest Madeira. We've got some in the cargo, just a few pipes of it, you understand. It's listed on the customs declaration."

The tide-waiters drank the wine, smacked their lips, pronounced it excellent, and departed without so much as a peek at the "Liberty's" cargo. This procedure was not unusual. Tide-waiters were often bribed to "forget" to check a vessel's cargo against its customs declaration. But soon everyone in the shipping trade in Boston heard the story that the "Liberty" had not brought just a few pipes of Madeira but was chock-a-block with it under her hatches.

The Sons of Liberty heard another story, too. One of their spies who knew his way about the customhouse told them, "Benjamin Hallowell, the comptroller of customs, is going to seize the 'Liberty' for smuggling in Madeira."

At about six o'clock on the evening of June 10, 1768, everything was quiet on Hancock's Wharf in the North End. The tall-masted "Liberty" lay silently at her moorings, save for an occasional lazy creak of her lines as she stirred slightly under the incoming tide. Her cargo had already been discharged—by night to keep it from prying eyes—and she was now loaded with tar and whale oil, ready for another voyage.

A small sailboat came alongside Hancock's Wharf, and two men stepped out and boarded the "Liberty." One was Benjamin Hallowell. The other, who carried an official-looking document and a hammer, was Joseph Harrison, a commissioner of customs.

Harrison walked up to the mainmast. There was a *rat-a-tat* of hammer blows as he nailed the document to the mast. It could not be read at a distance, but at the top of the paper a heavy black symbol stood out plainly:

It was the King's broad arrow, and it signified that the "Liberty" was now the property of the Crown.

By what seemed a strange coincidence, a large crowd suddenly appeared on the shore by the wharf. With a roar, the people began to hurl bricks, cobblestones, and clubs at the two customs officials on deck.

Hallowell and Harrison leaped to the wharf and ran for their lives. But when they reached the sailboat they were too late; several brawny, scowling men with bulging muscles were in possession of it. Ducking and dodging the barrage of missiles, the two officials dashed for the shore. A brick struck Hallowell, and he went down; an instant later Harrison was felled. But both men managed to get to their feet and flee up Fish Street to safety.

Then the mob surged onto the wharf, howling savagely. Some of the men seized the sailboat, hauled it out of the water, attached ropes to it, and dragged it through the town. When the crowd reached the Common the craft was set afire.

When the rest of the royal commissioners in Boston heard the news, they fled in terror with their families to the safety of Castle Island. But a day of reckoning was near for Boston. On September 30, 1768, it arrived.

On that fine fall morning, when people got out of bed and looked out of their windows toward the harbor, they saw a fleet of twelve ships anchored just off the Long Wharf at the foot of King Street. Towering ships of the line with three tiers of gunports pointed the ugly snouts of their cannon straight at the town. There were also smaller armed schooners and several transports.

Later that morning, as an endless stream of small boats, all jammed to the gunwales with soldiers in scarlet coats and white breeches, began to put off from the transports, the footways on each side of King Street were packed solid with people, and constables were holding them back with their pikestaffs.

From down the harbor, cannon on Castle Island thundered out a salute. Smoke and flame burst from the warships' guns as they returned it. Standing on tiptoe and craning their necks, the spectators on King Street could see the soldiers landing on the Long Wharf and forming ranks.

Then fifes began to play and drums rolled. The regiments marched up the slope in a great scarlet wave that engulfed King Street. The squealing of the fifes was like impish glee, as though they were laughing at these obstinate children of His Majesty George III who had had the impudence to twist the mighty British lion's tail. Each slam of the drums was like a hammer blow from the mailed fist of Britain.

On they came. The sun glinted on shouldered muskets, on buttons and gorgets, on the gold lace of the officers' uniforms, and on their drawn swords. It flashed on the brass of cannon, too, for there was a train of artillery with the troops.

A frightened whisper ran through the crowd: "They say they've given every redcoat sixteen rounds of powder and ball!" But for the most part the people watched in silence as the regiments tramped by, a thousand white-clad legs moving as one. Soldiers . . . soldiers armed with muskets . . . right in Boston . . . !

Two full regiments, part of another, and the artillery arrived that day, and still more troops appeared a week later. By that time there were four thousand soldiers in Boston, almost one to every four inhabitants.

Something terrible and tragic was coming. Soon Samuel Adams, who had turned all his energies toward bringing independence to America, was to see an incensed people rise in rebellion, bringing them to the very brink of war.

Chapter 7

FOR A TIME no serious incidents occurred. It was fortunate that some of the patriot leaders were level-headed enough to see the danger of rash action at this time. Otherwise, James Otis and other hot-tempered Whigs might have encouraged the mob to unleash its fury at the redcoats. Samuel Adams was one of those who favored caution, and his words carried weight in Boston.

It had been learned ahead of time that the troops were being sent from Halifax, even though the governor had tried to conceal the fact. About two weeks before they arrived, a special town meeting had been held in Faneuil Hall in Dock Square.

When the meeting began, James Otis was elected to preside as moderator. He came to the platform, faced the audience, and pointed dramatically toward one corner of the hall. The people, craning their necks for a better view, saw four hundred muskets stacked against the wall.

"There is an old law of this province requiring every citizen to have a musket, a pound of powder, and a pound of bullets ready for use when danger threatens," Otis began. "I ask you to vote arms for Boston according to this law. Then these muskets will be given out to all who need them."

His words threw the meeting into an uproar. All over the hall men rose, shouting demands that the colony fight as soon as the troops arrived. One shouted, "Kill them! Kill all the redcoats!"

Then Samuel Adams, shrewd and farsighted as usual, got up and came forward. He stood before the people with his hand raised for silence. "I ask you to vote that next Tuesday be set aside as a day of prayer," he said gravely, "that we may all ask divine aid against the wrongs we are suffering."

Silence fell over the meeting, and the people voted to hold the day of prayer. Sam's suggestion had set a keynote for the town. They would not fight. They would have dignity, let the British soldiers remain, and pray for God's deliverance. And for the most part, for more than a year, the people suffered the redcoats' presence in sullen silence.

It was not easy. There were soldiers everywhere. They marched and drilled all over town and at all hours, even before people were up in the morning. The infernal din of their squealing fifes and thundering drums, the slam of their musket butts on the pavement as they came to order arms, seemed to echo from one end of Boston to the other. Taverns were jammed with redcoats. Sometimes, on the streets, when people did not get out of the way fast enough, the soldiers shouldered them aside or jabbed at them with their bayonets.

The British officers were haughty, and in the market they used their authority to buy the best cuts of meat and the freshest fish, leaving the housewives to make do with what was left.

Until cold weather came, most of the soldiers camped on the Common. There, quite often, horrified citizens saw men triced up to a whipping post, screaming as the vicious cat-o'-nine-tails whistled down on their bare and bleeding backs in punishment for some small offense.

What Boston hated most was that the main guard of the army was stationed in a building near the head of King Street. In front of it, cannon had been wheeled up and pointed directly at the State House, originally called the Town House, where the House of Representatives held its sessions.

There were periodic disturbances, of course. In the taverns, fights started between redcoats and Bostonians. Small boys who had heard their parents speak bitterly of the soldiers, taunted them with yells of "Lobster!" and "Bloodyback!" and let fly from behind fences with spoiled fruit, rotten eggs, and oyster shells.

The soldiers had at least one four-footed enemy, too. Not only were all the members of Sam Adams' household stanch patriots like himself, but Queue, the huge Newfoundland dog, took a special dislike to redcoats. When one of them once tried to make friends by offering him a piece of meat, Queue, being a true patriot and preferring soldier to pork, bit him. After that he kept a sharp eye out for the sight of a scarlet uniform, never missing a chance to snarl and snap at the man wearing it. Soldiers used savage kicks and bayonet thrusts to fight him off and sometimes even shot at him, but Queue bore a charmed life and escaped with nothing more than a few scars on his shaggy hide.

Even though there were no overt signs of rebellion, the Sons of Liberty were busy. The patriot merchants of Boston and New York had decided to boycott British goods as long as the Townshend Act was in force. Those of Philadelphia, another great seaport, soon joined them. A good many of the merchants, however, were Tories who sided with the Crown. These men the Sons of Liberty frightened into joining what was called the Nonimportation Agreement. A close watch was kept on such merchants to see that they did not violate the agreement.

No one knew what else went on at the Sons of Liberty meetings, but at about that time British soldiers began to desert. It happened often enough to worry the officers; so General Thomas Gage, commander in chief of the British forces in America, who had come to Boston from his headquarters in New York when the troops arrived, was forced to take stern measures to stop it.

One day a deserter was caught and immediately court-martialed and sentenced to death. At dawn the next morning the regiments were paraded on the Common to watch the execution. The prisoner was marched out, tied to a post, and blindfolded. The drums beat a long roll as a firing squad took aim, and at an officer's command a volley roared and echoed over Boston. This episode shocked and appalled the people far more than the whippings, but it did not put an end to the desertions. The story got about that the Sons of Liberty were losing no chances to tell the redcoats how pleasant life could be in America once they got away from the British army with its weevilly biscuit, rotten pork, whippings, and executions.

Sam Adams did his part to show the redcoats that the Americans were humane and good-hearted people. Punishment in the British army was so brutal that soldiers sometimes died after a vicious whipping. One day the wife of an enlisted man who had come to Boston to be with him called on Samuel Adams.

"My husband has been sentenced to three hundred lashes," she sobbed. "He will surely die if he receives them. You are a man of great influence, Mr. Adams. Please help me, sir."

"I will go to General Gage and see what I can do," Sam promised gravely.

He went up to Province House, the official residence of the royal governors of Massachusetts Bay and now also General Gage's headquarters. It was an imposing three-story brick building with a cupola on top of which was a weathervane, the bronze figure of an Indian fitting an arrow to his bow.

The patriot leader's arrival must have caused quite a sensation, with much saluting and clicking of heels by redcoated guards and orderlies as he was escorted to General Gage's office. It would have been interesting to see and hear what went on when those two men faced each other.

One might have thought that they could scarcely

have been less alike—Gage, erect and military in his immaculate, tight-laced scarlet coat, and poorly clad, aging Sam Adams with his stoop and the tremor in his hands and voice. Yet everyone in Boston had noticed their resemblance to one another. They were nearly of the same age, and while they would not have been mistaken for twins, they might well have been brothers.

There is no official account of their meeting, but it is certain that their conversation was affable and courteous. Though they did not do so to his face, General Gage's officers affectionately called him Tommy. Everyone—even the people of Boston—liked him, though some of the younger officers thought him a little too grandmotherly for a commander in chief. But all agreed he was a fine fellow.

Sam left Province House with Gage's promise to spare the British soldier a lashing. No doubt the general had his reasons. Since he recognized Samuel Adams as one of the most dangerous enemies he had to face in his task of preventing an uprising in Boston, it would have served no purpose to antagonize the patriot.

As for Sam, it would be nice to think that he went to Gage simply out of the goodness of his heart, for a great and kindly heart he had. But if it was true that the Sons of Liberty were actively encouraging British soldiers to desert, Samuel Adams knew about it and was anxious to help the cause along. The redcoats of Gage's army would certainly hear how a patriot leader had saved one of their comrades from a brutal lashing and perhaps death.

Sam was using his pen in another direction now.

He had started a newspaper, the *Journal of Events,* which contained almost nothing but stories of "atrocities" Bostonians were suffering at the hands of the soldiers. They beat up small boys. They desecrated the Sabbath by carousing, firing guns, and having horse races. Their actions toward decent girls and women were shameful. So said the *Journal of Events.*

A good many of the stories were probably true. Some of the soldiers were nice enough young fellows, but many of the British army's enlisted men in those days were riffraff and ne'er-do-wells. One of the regiments, the Twenty-ninth, had more than its share of "gallows birds," as these rascals were called. On the other hand, soldiers were often provoked into retaliation by the taunts and missiles of the townspeople. And just as a clever rewrite man on a newspaper today can often turn what is really a rather dull story into an exciting one, so Sam Adams could make the stories in the *Journal of Events* sound so shocking that people gasped in horror as they read them.

Meanwhile, something happened which made Boston very happy; Francis Bernard was finally recalled to England. On the day the hated governor set sail for London, the bells of Boston rang out as joyously as they had at the news of the Stamp Act repeal. Flags were flown, cannon were fired, and an immense bonfire flamed up on Fort Hill.

Officially, Bernard was still governor, but actually the people of Massachusetts Bay found themselves ruled by a man they hated even more. Lieutenant Governor Thomas Hutchinson now became acting governor. He was especially unpopular just then because he and his two sons, all merchants, had refused to sign the Nonimportation Agreement and went right on buying English goods and offering them for sale. No one ever accused Thomas Hutchinson of being a coward.

There had still been no serious trouble in Boston, but as the winter of 1769-1770 drew toward its close, the people were becoming more short-tempered and irritable every day. Between the sly schemes of the Sons of Liberty and Sam Adams' vividly colored stories in the *Journal of Events,* they had been inflamed to a point where only a spark was needed to touch off an explosion. Early in March, 1770, something happened that struck the spark.

It began on March 2, not a stone's throw from Samuel Adams' house, at John Gray's ropewalk, the long, low-roofed shed that had intrigued Sam as a boy. About eleven o'clock that morning, dinner hour for the hands, two British soldiers walked into one of the sheds.

"Is there any work to be 'ad 'ere?" one of them, a private named Kilroy, asked.

Colonel Dalrymple, who was in command of the troops now that General Gage had gone back to New York, allowed the soldiers to do odd jobs in their spare time. Because the Nonimportation Agreement had brought trade almost to a standstill, times were hard in Boston. It enraged the people to see redcoats, who drew their pay regularly, taking jobs that their own needy citizens might have had.

Sam Gray, a lantern-jawed journeyman who was no relation to the ropewalk owner, was sitting on a bench eating his dinner. He growled out a coarse answer, specifying the kind of dirty work he would like to see the Britisher doing.

The offensive reply angered the soldier, and he started toward the journeyman, who leaped up. With raised fists the two men started to circle each other warily like a couple of snarling dogs. Meanwhile Kilroy's companion dashed out and hurried to some nearby barracks to rally supporters.

Some of the other ropewalk hands picked up clubs and closed in on Kilroy, who backed his way to the door. As he reached it he shouted, "I'll 'ave satisfaction for this! I'm not afraid of you in a fair fight!"

As he started to walk off, a ropewalker followed him and knocked him down. Just then Kilroy's friend returned with seven or eight more soldiers, all armed with clubs. A furious battle began. Outnumbered as they were, the redcoats gave a good account of themselves until the ropewalk owner appeared, ordered his men back inside, and put an end to the brawl.

The soldiers, rubbing their bruises, shuffled off toward the barracks. One turned and looked back, shaking his fist at the ropewalkers. Blood was streaming from his nose.

"Yah!" he yelled. "You 'aven't seen the end o' this!" He drew his hand across his face and looked at it. "Blood," he muttered. "It's your own that'll be spilt next, and soon—aye, the streets'll run red with it, mind!"

The three days that followed were quiet in Boston, but it was an uneasy quiet. They were like the still, cloudless, midsummer days in the tropics that sailors call "weather breeders" because they herald the approach of a hurricane.

Snow fell on Monday, March 5, but that night it was clear and cold. Boston lay like a fairy-tale town under a bright moon. In the shadows the houses might have been made of gingerbread, with their snowy roofs sugar icing in which millions of tiny diamonds sparkled in the moonlight.

Suddenly the deep-voiced bell of the Old Brick Church began to clang, not in the measured strokes with which it struck the hours, but wildly, the way it rang for what Boston dreaded more than soldiers' bullets—fire.

Within minutes the streets were filled with dark figures muffled in cloaks and greatcoats against the cold. Most of them appeared to have no idea what had happened, but some seemed to know exactly what they were doing and they led the way toward Dock Square. Some of the people carried fire buckets and lanterns.

There was a confusion of shouting:

"Town born, turn out! Town born, turn out!"

"The whole South End's afire!"

"The redcoats are murdering the people!"

"They're cutting down the Liberty Tree!"

All over town, windows slammed up. Voices hoarse with sleep demanded, "Where's the fire?"

The crowd poured into Dock Square from all directions. But there was not a sign of fire. At one end of the square, however, in front of a crazy-looking building with so many gables that people called it the Old Cocked Hat, stood a figure talking to the crowd as it gathered about him. He was wrapped to the ears in a red cloak, and his three-cornered hat was pulled so low over his eyes that in the shadow of the Old Cocked Hat even those closest to him could not make out his face clearly.

Then he raised his arm, pointed, and ordered, "To the main guard!"

The mob took up the cry as it moved in the direction he had indicated. As the people edged toward King Street, they looked at each other, asking, "Who was the man in the red cloak?"

"It was Sam Adams," someone said. "Everybody knows Sam always wears a red cloak in winter."

"No, it wasn't," another stated just as positively. "It was too tall for Sam."

No one seemed to know. And by that time the mysterious red-cloaked figure was no longer to be seen. He had vanished in the shadows.

The crowd reached King Street, with still no sign of fire anywhere, but some of the men led the way straight down the street to the customhouse.

Stationed outside it, a British sentry stood motionless, his scarlet coat a bright splash against the snow. As the mob swarmed closer, someone hurled a snowball at the sentry and he ducked. More snowballs, oyster shells, and stones began to rain down on him amid shouts of "Get the lobster!" "Kill the bloodyback!"

The soldier retreated a step, trying to shield himself from the flying missiles. He was breathing hard, his eyes wild with fright. "Keep back!" he gasped. "Keep back, blast you, or I'll blow your brains out!"

Someone yelled, "Go ahead! Fire if you dare!"

The mob surged forward, and the redcoat backed up the customhouse steps. A snowball with a stone buried in its center missed the sentry and shattered with a sharp crack against the customhouse door.

Halting resolutely at the top step, the sentry loaded his musket, rammed the charge home, and primed the pan from his powder horn.

Just then an enormous mulatto pushed his way to the front. "Yah!" he snarled. "I'll have off one of your claws, lobster!"

There were shouts of "Huzza for Crispus Attucks!" "Get the lobster's claw, Crispus!"

"Turn out the main guard!" the sentry shouted.

A few moments later there was a commotion in the crowd. Seven British soldiers led by a young captain fought their way to the sentry and formed a half circle about him.

By that time the uproar in King Street was so deafening that no one heard the command the officer gave or the rattle of the soldiers' ramrods as they loaded.

A fat man struggled forward out of the crowd and went up to the officer. Someone cried, "It's young Knox. It's Henry Knox that's apprenticed to Daniel Henchman the bookseller. He's a militia officer."

Knox, who later became one of George Washington's generals, was shouting at the British officer, "I beg you, Captain, march your men back. If you fire, your life will answer for the consequences!"

The officer eyed him coldly. "I know what I'm about," he replied in his clipped British accent.

Another man pushed out of the crowd. "Are the guns loaded, Captain Preston?" he demanded.

"Aye, with powder and ball."

"Do you mean to fire on the inhabitants?"

"By no means."

Just then Crispus Attucks strode up to Captain Preston, raised his club, and swung. The British officer saw the blow coming and dodged. It glanced off the sentry's shoulder instead, knocking him off balance. As he went down, his gun fell into the snow, and both he and Attucks dived for it. In the scramble the sentry managed to retrieve his weapon.

Again the mob pressed forward. Above its howling came an order: "Present!"

Those in the forefront halted in their tracks, staring into the menacing black holes of the gun muzzles. The sentry, who had lost his hat in the scuffle, had his musket aimed straight at Crispus Attucks, who stood there with a puzzled expression as if he could not believe what he saw.

Now a deathly silence fell over King Street. Some in the crowd later claimed that they clearly heard an order, though they could not tell who gave it: "Fire!"

Flame and smoke exploded from the sentry's musket. Its blast was followed by an unearthly scream as Crispus Attucks fell writhing into the snow. The rest of the guard fired into the crowd. The sentry quickly reloaded his musket and discharged it point-blank into Attucks' body. The mulatto stopped moving and lay still.

The scene in King Street was an ugly one. Motionless figures lay sprawled out in the trampled, blood-stained snow. Still others thrashed about, moaning. One man, wounded in the leg, tried to rise, sank back, and then began to drag himself away, inch by inch. The subdued mob milled around, trying to push its way out of King Street to safety.

The Boston Massacre was over.

✑ Chapter 8 ✑

FOUR MEN LAY dead in front of the customhouse. Eight others were wounded. One of those killed was Sam Gray. By a strange coincidence he had been at the front of the mob, while Kilroy, the redcoat who had asked for work, was one of the soldiers with Captain Preston. Kilroy had not forgotten Gray's insult. When he saw the ropewalker in the crowd, he took deliberate aim and shot him. Then he thrust his bayonet through Gray's lifeless body.

Captain Preston, appalled at what had happened, struck up his soldiers' muskets, shouting, "Hold your fire!"

Once the crowd saw that there would be no more firing, courage returned, and they stopped trying to flee from King Street. Instead, they turned back and howled for vengeance.

All over Boston, in the barracks and warehouses where the soldiers were quartered for the winter, drums were beating a call to arms. Companies marched into King Street and halted, facing the mob. It looked very much as though there would be more shooting after all, with even more terrible consequences.

Once again Thomas Hutchinson showed his courage. At his mansion in North Square, he heard the volley and set out at once. Somehow he managed to fight his way safely through the ugly-tempered mob to the State House. Going up to the second floor, he walked out on a balcony that faced King Street.

He stood with his hand held up for silence, and at length the mob's caterwauling died down.

"Disperse!" he pleaded. "Let the law take its course and settle this thing. Go home peaceably, and I promise you that an inquiry will be held in the morning."

"We want action now!" a man in the crowd yelled. "Arrest Preston! Get the soldiers off the streets!"

The acting governor shook his head. "I have no authority over the troops," he replied. "That is up to Colonel Dalrymple."

At his words the mob set up a menacing cry and surged forward toward the State House.

Just then Lieutenant Colonel Dalrymple appeared on the balcony. "If you agree, Your Excellency," he said, "I will have one of the companies escort Captain Preston and his men to the jail, where they will be safe. Otherwise, the mob will surely tear them to pieces. Preston has already been badly mauled. Meanwhile I will have the rest of the troops marched to their quarters." And as Hutchinson nodded, Dalrymple gave the necessary orders. Satisfied, the mob went home.

By his calmness and courage in an emergency, Hutchinson probably prevented the start of a full-scale rebellion then and there. If it had begun then, it would have been put down quickly. Even though the colonies were fairly well united when the Revolution broke out in 1775, they had little enough chance to win. It is one of the great miracles of history that they did.

Captain Preston and his men were not allowed to leave the jail in the morning. After the British officer had been questioned all night, he and the eight soldiers were charged with murder.

All Boston was seething. To commemorate the event Paul Revere, an engraver and silversmith by trade and American patriot by choice, made an engraving of the Massacre that became famous. The Sons of Liberty immediately sent couriers galloping through the countryside to ask for arms and help from the outlying villages. Soon many men carrying muskets began to flock into Boston. There was still great danger that violence might flare up at any moment.

Everyone seemed to have his own story of what had happened in King Street, and none of them agreed very well. Nor was there any agreement as to who the mysterious figure in a red cloak had been. Those who had gotten close enough to hear him said that he had incited the mob to violence. But while some insisted it had been Sam Adams, others were just as sure it was not. Many thought it had been Will Molineux, another ardent patriot.

Was it Sam Adams? It would appear to be doubtful, and for a good reason. He might lay plans and pull strings, but he was careful not to give his enemies any open cause to bring charges of treason against him. He never participated actively in any of the other mob disturbances that took place in Boston before the Revolution. He attended town meetings and mass public meetings, yes. But when it came to rioting, he let others act—especially Will Molineux, whom the Tories sneeringly called the Sons of Liberty's "First Leader in Dirty Matters."

Molineux was a middle-aged merchant who had made a moderate fortune dealing in hardware. But along with other merchants after the Nonimportation Agreement went into effect, he had fallen on hard times. Being a rough, hot-tempered Irishman, he naturally blamed the British for his difficulties and was determined to have revenge. One of the most active members of the Sons of Liberty, he was always on hand when there was trouble brewing.

The morning after the Boston Massacre there was an immense mass meeting at Faneuil Hall. Samuel Adams arose and told the people that Governor Hutchinson had already refused a demand by the selectmen that the troops be removed from Boston, again claiming that he had no authority to do so. Sam was elected head of a committee of fifteen to go to the governor and warn him to get the soldiers out of town if he hoped to avoid more bloodshed.

At three o'clock that afternoon the people went back to Faneuil Hall to hear the committee's report. By that time so many country folk had flooded into Boston that the crowd would not fit into the hall. The meeting was adjourned to the larger Old South Meetinghouse, but even that was not big enough.

Outside the church a cry of, "Make way for the

committee!" went up, and the rest of the crowd that had been unable to get in parted to let Samuel Adams and the others through. In his red cloak Sam led them, bareheaded and wigless, his gray hair streaming in the wind, for the day was blustery, with a slate-gray sky that promised more snow.

Inside the meetinghouse every pew was taken and the aisles were jammed. A buzz of excitement rose quickly in the church as the committee threaded its way to the front, but it died to a tense hush when Samuel Adams faced the people from the platform.

"The governor," Sam told them, "regrets the unhappy differences which have arisen between the citizens and the soldiers." He paused significantly, and angry snorts sounded from the audience. Then he continued, "His Excellency informed the committee that since General Gage, who is now in New York, gave orders that the troops be quartered in the town, he cannot countermand those orders."

Sam let the rumblings subside before he went on, "However, the governor added that the Twenty-ninth Regiment will be transferred to the fort on Castle Island, the Fourteenth Regiment restrained, and the main guard removed."

Once more he paused for a long moment. "Is this satisfactory?" he then demanded. "Is the removal of one regiment enough? What is your answer?"

In the packed meetinghouse a roar went up from three thousand throats: *"No!"*

Samuel Adams bowed his head gravely in acknowledgment. "Your committee will return to the Council chamber and demand the total evacuation of the troops from the town." And with the others he set out again for the State House.

Outside, the overflow from the mass meeting stood silently, paying no heed to the snow that had begun to fall. The committee passed them and plodded through Cornhill with its many shops. Reaching King Street, Samuel Adams and the others ascended the steps leading to the Council chamber at the east end of the building.

From the doorway the committee could look directly into the square, pillared chamber. In the gloom of the late afternoon, the light of the blaze in the fireplace played upon the twenty-eight members of the Council seated about a long, oval table. They had thrown their scarlet cloaks aside, revealing gorgeous raiment, some in blue, others in red, plum, or green. Their three-cornered hats, which they had placed on the table, were laced with gold. There they sat in full dress, wearing swords and powdered wigs.

At the head of the table sat Governor Hutchinson in crimson; on his right hand, Lieutenant Colonel Dalrymple, clad in the scarlet, white, and gold of His Majesty's Army. Directly behind them, in the flickering illumination of the firelight, the committee could see full-length oil paintings of two of England's Stuart kings in their royal robes of ermine and purple.

One was Charles II, dark-eyed, handsome, slim, and graceful as a woman, wearing his glossy, curling black wig. His stern expression gave no hint of the love for life's pleasures and good living which had earned him the name of "the Merry Monarch," nor of the smile that drew his subjects to him and made him their idol. Beside him, long-faced, thin-lipped James II gazed out upon the Council chamber with all the austerity and meanness that had made him known as "Dismal Jimmy."

Francis Bernard had hung the paintings there—one of the things Boston hated him for. Just to look at them was enough to make any Puritan bristle. These brother kings had come to the throne after the Commonwealth era, when there had been no King and England had been ruled by a Protector, the Puritan Oliver Cromwell. And one of the many names Samuel Adams acquired during his lifetime was that of "the Last of the Puritans."

Sam walked straight toward the long table, followed by the rest of the committee. He had taken off his cloak, and as he stood before the Council, a stooped figure in an old, crumpled coat, he made a strange contrast with the scene of pomp and splendor. Yet every eye was on him. It was as if they knew that this shabby man held the people of Boston in the palm of his hand and that his decision would be theirs.

For all its palsied quaver, his voice was clear and commanding:

"It is the unanimous opinion of the meeting that the reply to the vote of the inhabitants during the morning is by no means satisfactory. Nothing less will satisfy them than a total and immediate removal of the troops."

Governor Hutchinson's lips were set firmly. "The troops are not subject to my authority," he replied. "I have no power to remove them."

Adams drew himself erect. His blue eyes, fixed

97

directly upon the governor, were flashing. He raised his arm and pointed a quivering finger at Hutchinson. "If you have the power to remove *one* regiment, you have power to remove *both*," he said.

As Sam waited for a reply, a movement under the table caught his eye. He saw that Hutchinson's knees were trembling. "I enjoyed the sight," he wrote later to a friend. And well he might have, if he recalled the day, while he was still a student at Harvard College, when his father had informed him of the failure of the Land Bank. The Hutchinsons had been largely responsible. Now Sam was delivering an ultimatum to one of them.

Seeing the governor's trembling, Samuel Adams pressed his advantage. "It is at your peril that you refuse," he continued. "There are three thousand people at the meeting. They are impatient. A thousand men have already come in from the country. Fifteen thousand are ready to rise throughout the province. Both regiments or none!"

The governor turned to Lieutenant Colonel Dalrymple, and the two held a whispered conference. Then Hutchinson nodded grimly to Samuel Adams. "Inform the people that their petition is granted," he said. "Colonel Dalrymple will begin preparations to remove the two regiments to the Castle in the morning."

Sam Adams bowed politely, turned, nodded to the committee, and they left the Council chamber.

He had won the greatest victory of his career. What would he have done if the governor had refused? No one can say. It was true that many of the country people would have joined the citizens of Boston if an uprising had started. Perhaps not fifteen thousand, but probably enough to drive the redcoats out, even though they were trained soldiers. But Samuel Adams knew that, as a result, many more British soldiers would have been sent to Boston.

Undoubtedly Sam was confident that he could force the governor to yield. Confidence is the most useful thing a man can have when he faces another in a crisis.

For the moment, at least, the danger of outright rebellion had passed. Two days later, while the church bells tolled slowly and mournfully, a huge, solemn funeral procession was formed. It started at the scene of the Massacre in front of the customhouse, which people were now calling Butcher's Hall. While it was not directly on the way to the burying ground, the procession took a route that led into Queen Street and past the jail where Captain Preston and the eight soldiers were imprisoned. But there was no disturbance.

There was a procession of quite a different kind a short while later. The two Boston regiments marched down King Street to the Long Wharf and embarked in boats that took them to the island fort in the harbor. And Boston, glad to have something to be merry about once more, made a holiday of it. Alongside Lieutenant Colonel Dalrymple at the head of the long column of glum-faced soldiers marched Will Molineux, leading some of the Sons of Liberty. Wearing a red and blue uniform, the patriot displayed the dress of no regiment that ever existed, but it was impressive all the same.

He wore his three-cornered hat at an insolent angle and kept sweeping it off in exaggerated bows to the spectators. Small boys raced up and down, mimicking the cadence of the marching feet, "Hup! Hup! Hup!" and yowling, "Lobsters! Who'll buy lobsters?" The watching crowd grinned and jeered.

Everybody except the redcoats had a wonderful time. In London, when the Prime Minister heard about it, he called them "Sam Adams' two regiments."

Meanwhile, two of the eight men who had been wounded in the Massacre died, making six in all who had been killed. And now people were talking about the trial of Captain Preston and the soldiers, for a startling thing had happened.

Earlier, Sam Adams had persuaded his cousin John to move with his family from the village of Braintree to Boston, where he practiced law and began to engage in politics with Sam. He soon became an active and important member of the Whig party, which favored colonial freedom. The day after the Massacre a friend of Captain Preston came to John Adams, explaining that the British army officer had no lawyer to defend him. The Crown's attorneys refused to touch the case, fearing that they might be mobbed. Preston needed counsel desperately—his very life was at stake. Would John Adams defend him? Sam's "brother Adams," along with his partner, Josiah Quincy, Jr., agreed to take the case. People could not understand it—two patriot lawyers defending this murderer who was an officer of the Crown! The very thought of it made them angry. John Adams and Quincy were jeered in the streets.

Samuel Adams, however, made no objection, for he was quick to realize the advantage of having them defend Captain Preston. Their role in the trial would preserve the reputation of Boston—and also protect the instigators of the Massacre. Many people were convinced that Sam had been the man in the red cloak who had urged the mob to attack the sentry. And even today there are those who claim that Adams feared the possibility of having incriminating evidence come out at the trial and that his cousin John was able to save him by keeping out such testimony. Without actual proof to show that Samuel Adams plotted the mischief, no one will ever know exactly what part he took in it. But one thing is certain, Sam approved of the defense lawyers and during the trial praised their handling of the case, in the newspapers.

He was unhappy about one thing, however; the court case was postponed for six months. Every defense lawyer knows the advantage of having an accused man's trial delayed. For one thing, it gives the public time to cool off. Sam may not have wanted a revolt to break out at that time, but neither did he want the memory of the Massacre to fade. He worked very hard to prevent the postponement, heading a town committee to demand that Hutchinson and the judges take early action. But his efforts proved unsuccessful, and by the time the trial took place in October of 1770 the public had lost considerable interest in it. The jury acquitted Captain Preston, a decision that disappointed Sam Adams and many Sons of Liberty. Later, when the eight soldiers were tried, with the same lawyers defending them, six were acquitted. Kilroy and the sentry who had killed

Crispus Attucks were found guilty of manslaughter, but even they were let off easily, being branded on the thumb with a red-hot iron. This was light punishment indeed, when in England poor women were often hanged for stealing a loaf of bread.

Strangely enough, on the very day of the Boston Massacre something happened that made Samuel Adams' task of keeping the people aroused against England much harder. As a result of it, patriot resistance to the Crown would have collapsed altogether but for him. On March 5, 1770, the detested Townshend Act was repealed.

Not entirely, however. Largely to remind America of its right to tax the colonies, Parliament left a single tax, the one on tea, in effect. England could not have made a worse mistake. Because of it, the biggest tea party in all history would be held, and to Englishmen the taste of the tea that was served would be very bitter indeed.

For a long time, however, no one paid much attention to it. Somehow the Massacre seemed to have sobered not only Boston but all of the American colonies. Certain patriots began to say that there was no reason why America should not get along better with England. When the Stamp Act and the Townshend Act had proved objectionable to the colonies, they had been repealed, hadn't they? Surely, if Parliament would be as reasonable in the future, their differences could be settled.

During the summer of 1770 merchants in New

York announced that they were giving up the Non-importation Agreement. Soon afterward those in the ports of Philadelphia and Charleston also abandoned it. That left only Boston, and now the merchants there grew restless. Why should they be the only ones to lose money? One of the first of them to end the boycott was John Hancock. He boldly put an advertisement in the Boston *Gazette* announcing that his sloop "Lydia" had arrived with a cargo of British goods, which he would sell at his shop. That was the beginning of the end for the Nonimportation Agreement in Massachusetts Bay. Hancock lost interest in the patriot cause, and it would be two years before he returned to it.

John Adams, too, lost interest after Sam wrote a series of articles for the Boston *Gazette* in which he bitterly attacked the outcome of the trials of Captain Preston and the soldiers. Although John was deeply offended and hurt, he did not let it interfere with his affection for Sam. He understood his cousin too well. "Sam Adams lives for the cause," he told his wife. "For it, I believe he would take his daughter and throw her in Boston Bay." He was joking, of course, but he knew how devoted Sam was to American liberty. Nevertheless, John reluctantly withdrew from politics, gave up his Boston law practice, and took his family back to Braintree.

Even the once-dedicated James Otis questioned whether total colonial independence was the best and wisest choice. The patriots began to feel that he could no longer be trusted to keep party secrets. When Thomas Hutchinson, who had been appointed governor after Bernard's recall in 1771, ordered the House of Representatives to meet in Cambridge instead of the rebellious town of Boston, Otis agreed with Hutchinson. He defended the governor's right to send the House to meet in Housatonic, on the western frontier of the province, if he saw fit to do so.

In a short time Samuel Adams was the only important patriot leader left. It began to look very much as if the troubles with England would be forgotten, but he was still convinced that sooner or later the colonies would have to break away. He continued to work, all the harder now, flooding the newspapers with letters signed with a dozen different pen names.

Even though the tax on tea worried no one very much in the ensuing period of good will toward England, Sam used it as the best available means of attack. "We can easily avoid paying the tribute by abstaining from the use of those articles by which it is extorted from us," he said in a newspaper article, using such words as "tribute" and "extorted" when he might have said "customs duty" and "collected," to remind the people of their bondage to the Crown.

"The body of the people are uneasy at the large strides that are made and making towards an absolute tyranny. Many are alarmed, but are of different sentiments with regard to the next step to be taken. Some, indeed, think that every step has been taken *but one,*" he wrote. Actually, there was little uneasiness at that time, nor was anyone but Sam Adams thinking of that last step, which was revolution. But he was sowing seeds.

Sometimes he boldly told the people that they were slaves who did not have the courage to rebel. Signing himself "Candidus," he wrote in the Boston *Gazette*: "I believe no people ever yet groaned under the heavy yoke of slavery but when they deserved it. If, therefore, people will not be free, if they have not virtue enough to maintain their liberty against a presumptuous invader, they deserve no pity, and are to be treated with contempt and ignominy."

At this time many of Samuel Adams' readers may have remarked, "Old Sam's the only man who's out of step these days. Why doesn't he see that no one wants any more trouble with England?" And probably Sam knew perfectly well that people were talking that way. But he did not care what they said—as long as they read what he wrote.

One person *was* worried about Sam Adams—Governor Hutchinson. Things were going along very nicely for him at that time. He was getting along with the people, other government officials, and even the House of Representatives. The only exception was Adams. Sam did not restrict himself to articles denouncing the Crown; he also attacked the governor. Undoubtedly he would have done so even if the Hutchinson family had not been involved in the Land Bank collapse. But it seems clear that Sam's personal grudge against the governor made the attacks even more bitter. It was Adams' way of striking back, not with fists but with words as sharp as little pricking needles.

Everyone will agree that the prick of one needle does not hurt very much, but when there are thousands of them that never stop jabbing, they can goad a man to fury. And at last they did. In a rage Governor Hutchinson sent to England a copy of the Boston *Gazette* containing one of Sam's denunciatory attacks on him. With the newspaper he enclosed a letter, stating that the article, signed with one of Sam's pen names, was in "the language of the Chief Incendiary of the House."

Chief Incendiary. Of all the uncomplimentary names the Tories called Sam Adams—and there were many of them—this was the most expressive. Thomas Hutchinson was no mean writer himself. The best history of Massachusetts Bay published in those times was written by the governor. He, too, knew how to turn a phrase.

By accusing Samuel Adams of lighting a fire of revolt, Hutchinson never wrote or spoke more truly. The fire of opposition to the Crown was burning very low at that point. But just as it flickered and seemed about to die out, there was Sam Adams blowing on it with all his might.

It did not go out.

✑ Chapter 9 ✑

IN HIS SINGLE-MINDED fight for the cause of liberty, Samuel Adams had lost the support of a number of influential leaders. Except for John Hancock, however, he had not lost the friendship of these men. They simply did not agree with him any longer. But for a reason other than politics he lost an old and powerful friend.

James Otis' enemies had long ago labeled him eccentric; now he became irritable and surly. Even his friends could never tell whether he would be his genial self or flare up in unprovoked anger. Sometimes he was seen walking the streets, muttering to himself.

More and more he began to associate with Crown officials and the British army officers who often came into Boston from Castle Island. The British Coffee House on King Street was a favorite gathering place for these men. One evening in the tavern someone questioned Otis' loyalty to the King. A bitter argument developed, ending in a fight in which everyone became involved. Furniture was smashed and the candles knocked over and put out. In the melee someone struck Otis a severe blow on the head that left a deep wound and cracked his skull.

From then on, Otis' behavior grew stranger and more unpredictable. He had been very popular with the people of Boston, and many felt sympathetic toward him in spite of his oddities. Sam, who had always had a special affection for him, even though the two were so different, now felt gravely concerned. He watched over Otis like a brother as it became apparent that the man's mind was affected.

One spring evening in 1770 Otis went upstairs in his house, threw open a window, and fired six shots through it. After each shot he gave a maniacal yell. A few days later Samuel Adams called at his friend's house and asked for him. The servant showed him into the sitting room where Otis was. No longer was he the burly, rampaging orator whom John Adams had called a "flame of fire." He had lost weight, his cheeks were hollow, and he looked like an old man. His eyes had a peculiar stare, but he greeted Sam affectionately. For a few minutes the two men sat chatting quietly; yet all the time it was as though Otis, despite his disordered mind, knew what was coming.

At last Sam said gently, "Jim, because we are good friends, I have been sent to tell you it is best that you resign from the House of Representatives."

James Otis nodded. "I understand, Sam," he muttered. "I shall do as they ask."

Samuel Adams' head was bowed when he left the house. It was one of the hardest things he had ever had to do. It would have an important effect on his future, too, though he was not thinking about that at the time.

And it would be a long while before he saw his friend again, for shortly afterward Otis became violent and was taken in a strait waistcoat to a place in the country.

Having lost one ally, Samuel Adams now regained another. John Hancock had not been able to make up his mind just where he stood in politics. Like many wealthy businessmen who had no grievances toward the Crown, he had been a loyal British subject. Sam had won him over to the colonists' cause during the trouble caused by Parliament's attempts to tax the colonies. After the repeal of the Townshend Act, Hancock decided that it was neither prudent nor profitable to align himself too strongly with either side, and he tried to steer a middle course without antagonizing the Whigs or the Tories. But it was impossible to straddle the political fence in Boston, and many considered him a Tory. In the spring of 1772 the patriots felt that Hancock and Adams should settle their differences and present a united front against the Crown.

Sam Adams was undoubtedly anxious to have John Hancock—and his fortune—safely back on his side. The wealthy merchant, meanwhile, had hopes of his own—to secure himself a strong political position in the government. His desire to play a popular, man-of-the-people role probably led him to choose the patriot party. Whatever their reasons, the two men made peace, and, to show that they were friends again, Hancock commissioned John Singleton Copley, his neighbor on Beacon Hill, to paint their portraits.

About this time Sam Adams decided that the moment had come to put into action an idea that had been in the back of his mind for a long while. With the support of his fellow representatives, he thought he could get the people of Boston to approve it. He succeeded in having a special town meeting called on November 2, 1772. In Faneuil Hall he stood before the people and told them his idea. In Boston, he said, the inhabitants knew what was being done to preserve their liberties. But other people outside heard little about it, especially in the remote villages to the west.

"I move," said Adams, "that a Committee of Correspondence be appointed, to consist of twenty-one persons, to state the rights of the colonists, and of this province in particular, and to communicate and publish the same to the several towns, with the infringements and violations thereof that have been or from time to time may be made."

His motion was adopted unanimously, and his inspired plan to let other towns know what was going on was put into effect with little delay. The letters were circulated only in Massachusetts Bay at first, but the Committee of Correspondence idea soon spread to other colonies, and they began to exchange letters with one another. These committees did a great deal to unify the American colonies—something very close to Sam Adams' heart.

Meanwhile Sam was busy in another way; he was still looking for a weapon powerful enough to destroy Thomas Hutchinson. Pricking him with needles was all very well, but Adams was searching for bigger ammunition, something more like a cannon ball. And oddly enough, it was Hutchinson himself who dropped it right in his lap.

Now Samuel Adams, who always did things cleverly, carefully prepared the way by first writing a number of letters in the Boston *Gazette,* hinting that something frightful was about to be revealed to the people. His ominous tone was remarkably effective in building up suspense and tension, as he intended that it should. When he felt that he had baited the readers long enough, he fired the cannon ball. Unerringly it found its target and wreaked its damage.

Readers of the *Gazette* avidly read the news one morning that the House of Representatives had charged Thomas Hutchinson and Andrew Oliver, formerly the unfortunate stamp master and now lieutenant governor, with serious offenses against the colonies. In a set of resolutions passed in the House, these two men were being held responsible for the writs of assistance, the Stamp Act, the Townshend Act, and the mobilization of redcoats in Boston. The proof was all in a series of letters that Hutchinson and Oliver had written to friends in the government in London. The resolutions were in the form of a petition to the King, asking His Majesty to remove Hutchinson and Oliver from office.

In the following issue of the *Gazette* the letters themselves were published. The readers of the newspaper gasped, bristled, and fumed as they read them. In this private correspondence Thomas Hutchinson had been off his guard and had said things he was going to wish he had never put on paper. So had Andrew Oliver.

Hutchinson had called the Boston selectmen ignorant. He had accused the people of voting measures that were criminal acts against the Crown. He had as good as accused them of cowardice, saying that when the troops had landed in Boston the people's bravado had weakened. And worst of all, he had said it was impossible for the people of the American colonies ever to have the same liberties as Englishmen in Britain. There were still more comments that made the readers of the *Gazette* seethe with anger.

How did Samuel Adams get hold of the letters and publish them? It is a strange story, filled with scheming and skulduggery. Dr. Benjamin Franklin was in London at this time, acting as one of the agents sent by the colonies to obtain favors they wanted from the government and to state their complaints. He not only represented the Pennsylvania colony, where he had gone from Boston as a boy, but also Massachusetts Bay.

Whether he would continue for long as the Bay colony's representative was doubtful. There was a good deal of criticism of Franklin in Boston. The patriot leaders thought he did altogether too much hobnobbing with nobility in London. They suspected that he was becoming Toryish. Wise old Dr. Franklin knew this and, anxious to keep his job and get back in the good graces of the Massachusetts leaders, somehow managed to get hold of a packet of the letters written by Hutchinson when he was lieutenant governor and by Oliver.

Franklin sent the letters to Tom Cushing, who was now speaker of the House of Representatives. Cushing was given permission to show them to Samuel Adams and to his cousin John, who had moved back to Boston, as well as to a few of the other leaders. But beyond that, Franklin directed, the letters were strictly confidential. Under no circumstances were they to be published.

We think of Benjamin Franklin as one of the wisest Americans of his time. How then can we believe that he expected these letters, so damaging to Thomas Hutchinson, to be kept secret? He surely knew that Sam Adams would let no chance slip to stir up trouble with England. And he knew, too, that Sam was Hutchinson's sworn enemy. It seems more likely that he realized perfectly well that the secret would come out but that he did not foresee how serious the consequences would be to himself.

It did not take Sam long to figure out a way to get around Franklin's order that the letters remain confidential. For published they had to be, if Hutchinson was to be ruined. Adams' solution to the problem was not subtle but it was effective—and it hinged on only one word. Franklin had been specific about *letters,* but he had said nothing about *copies* of them. . . .

John Hancock stood up before the House of Representatives, holding a batch of papers in his hand. A man had given them to him on Boston Common that morning, he said. It seemed that they were letters written by Hutchinson and Oliver.

One of the other leaders got up. "Letters written by His Excellency and Andrew Oliver have been received by Speaker Cushing," he said. "They have been turned over to Samuel Adams as clerk of the House. The ones Mr. Hancock has may be duplicates. I move that they be compared with the originals and that if they are true copies they be published."

Of course, everyone present knew that the letters so mysteriously handed to John Hancock were copies, but the story gave them their out.

That was the end of Thomas Hutchinson.

Although he remained governor for a time, his career in Boston was doomed. He had been hated by the poor, working-class people in the days when they had formed a mob to wreck his mansion, but now he was hated even by citizens who would have scorned to join a mob. As for Andrew Oliver, when he died less than a year later, his friends said that it was from a broken heart over the scandal.

When news of the publication of the correspondence reached London, Dr. Franklin was denounced on all sides. He was called "a viper festering in the bosom of government," "the old dotard," and "a skunk or American pole cat." The King, who had made him postmaster general of the American colonies, canceled the appointment.

It is impossible to admire Samuel Adams for what he did. True, Benjamin Franklin should never have sent the letters to Boston, but Sam betrayed his confidence on a pretext that anyone could see was a fraud. John Adams was right when he said that Sam lived solely for the cause.

Knowing him to be a loving husband and father, the kindly man many in Boston loved, it is hard to picture him as a crafty schemer, willing to use his friends for his own purposes and even to doublecross them. Nevertheless the fact remains; he devoted his entire life to winning American independence. Some may think that he was wrong to do the things he did to achieve it. But it is necessary to remember that he gave all he had for the cause and that he used whatever means came to hand in order to accomplish what he set out to do.

Samuel Adams now found himself the acknowledged leader of the patriots. Although James Otis had returned from the country, somewhat better, he would never again be able to resume a commanding position in politics.

As leader, Sam once more cast about for something he could use to rouse the people. He had destroyed Thomas Hutchinson, but relations between the colonies and England remained peaceful. The people's rage was directed largely against the governor and Oliver.

What Sam Adams needed was coming soon. And this time there would be no turning back.

❧ Chapter 10 ❧

ALMOST EVERYONE IN Boston was fond of tea. People drank a great deal of it, but not much came from England. Most of it was Dutch tea, smuggled in by John Hancock and other big merchant-shipowners. It was much cheaper that way.

And because not only Boston but other parts of the American colonies drank this smuggled tea, millions of pounds' worth of English tea lay in the warehouses of the great East India Company in London. It would rot if it was not purchased soon, and the company would be ruined. That meant that four hundred thousand pounds of revenue the government received from this tea trade would be lost.

Why not force America to buy it? To do so the leaders of the government devised a clever scheme. They granted certain concessions to the East India Company, making it possible to cut the price of tea in half. And only this company would be permitted to trade in it. Now, said the Crown officials, with English tea so much cheaper, no more Dutch tea would be smuggled into the colonies.

It was a fine idea, except that they left a customs duty of threepence a pound on English tea. If they had taken that off, there probably would have been no trouble. But as it was, they played right into Sam Adams' hand, for he had been attacking England over this "taxation without representation."

If John Hancock ever had any thought that he might change his mind again about colonial independence, it was gone now. He and others who had been smuggling Dutch tea were furious. Certain merchants had been appointed consignees to handle the tea trade in Boston for the East India Company, among them Governor Hutchinson's two sons, young Thomas and Elisha. Thus Hancock and the others would lose the profits from their contraband sales.

Nor were they the only ones who were alarmed. "Suppose," said merchants who dealt in such items as cloth and hardware, "the government decides to do the same thing with these goods. We will be ruined."

Sam Adams, of course, had been warning the colonists of such a possibility. All the patriot leaders were behind him, and now the people, angry at this scheme to force British tea down their throats, were ready to listen to him.

Through the Committees of Correspondence the leaders in Boston heard that the merchants and citizens of other colonies were also indignant and ready for action.

Meanwhile a fast ship reached Boston with news that slower vessels loaded with tea were on the way.

On November 1, 1773, notices were posted all over town summoning the inhabitants to a noonday mass meeting at the Liberty Tree. At the same time summonses were shoved under the doors of all the tea consignees, demanding that they come to the meeting and resign their appointments.

The people came, but the tea consignees did not. Hutchinson's sons had fled the town and were hiding at the governor's country place in the village of Milton.

Now a mystery developed. The Boston *Gazette* was printed by two patriots, Benjamin Edes and John Gill. Their office was on Queen Street, near the prison where Captain Preston and his soldiers had been confined after the Massacre. Passers-by on their way home from taverns late at night were surprised to see candles burning in the printing office. That seemed very strange. The printers of the weekly *Gazette* seldom had to work late. Obviously, something was going on, though what it was no one could guess, and the leaders of the Sons of Liberty who met there night after night kept their usual strict silence.

The first of the tea ships, the "Dartmouth," arrived on November 28. Her captain, fearing to bring his vessel up the harbor, anchored off Castle Island, where he was protected by the fort's cannon. Soon afterward, two more tea ships, the "Beaver" and the "Eleanor," arrived and dropped anchor near-by.

The candles continued to burn far into the night at the printing shop. . . .

Something had to happen by December 17. Under

the law, that was the last day the tea could remain in the port of Boston without paying duty. After that the customs authorities would have to seize it. The patriots could not allow that to happen, for then those officials could sell the tea secretly. And while no one in Boston would dare to buy it openly, there were plenty of Tories who would if no one knew about it.

On December 16 there was a meeting at the Old South Church. Young Henry Purkitt and Samuel Sprague, who were apprenticed to a cooper, were given permission to attend. Boston was a gray town, and on that afternoon it was dreary under a steady, cold drizzle. When the two boys reached the church, there was a great crowd milling about, all trying to get in. Henry and Sam pushed and shoved their way close to the door. Suddenly they were caught in a whirlpool of struggling humanity and swept inside the church.

The main floor was already packed to bursting, but like young eels the two boys wriggled through to the stairs and just managed to squeeze into one of the benches in the gallery. Henry Purkitt sat back for a moment, out of breath. Mingled with the musty church odor he had always thought of as God's smell, the steamy reek of water-soaked clothing reached his nose. He thought of all the people who had been unable to get in, standing there in the chill downpour, and he congratulated himself. For now, three-quarters of an hour before the start of the meeting, there was not one inch of sitting or standing room left.

Though it was still early afternoon, it was so dark

inside that Henry Purkitt, leaning forward in his seat, could see little of what was going on down on the main floor until the sexton of the church pushed through the side aisles and lighted candles in sconces on the walls. All at once the boxlike rectangles of the pews and the outline of the raised pulpit with its sounding board overhead sprang into detail. But even with the candle-light, much of the ground floor seemed to be just a blended, drab mass of gray homespun and leather. Here and there, however, bright patches stood out—a crim-son cloak, a canary-yellow coat, a white powdered wig, showing that not all of Boston's patriots were work-ingmen.

Beside Henry Purkitt, Sam Sprague raised his hand and waved to someone across the middle aisle of the gallery. "Hey, George, you rogue!" he called out. The other one waved back.

Henry looked over and saw a midget of a fellow, no bigger than himself, but a grown man all the same. There was an impish gleam in the runty one's eye, as though he knew some dark secret and could hardly wait for it to be disclosed.

"Who's he?" Henry demanded of his companion.

"That's George Robert Twelves Hewes. He's one of the Liberty Boys. Awful big name for such a little feller, ain't it?" Sam Sprague nodded wisely. "There'll be a rumpus of some kind before this thing's over. George can smell trouble a mile off."

Henry wondered how his companion happened to know Hewes. Sometimes he thought Sam Sprague knew a lot more than he was telling about the doings of the

Liberty Boys, as everyone called the Sons of Liberty.

The people in the Old South were quiet enough while they waited. There was a low buzz of conversation, but no excitement, and at last all sound died away suddenly.

"They're coming in," Sam Sprague said. "That's John Hancock leading 'em."

Craning his neck, Henry Purkitt leaned forward. He saw the crowd in the aisle give way respectfully before a tall, slim, delicately handsome figure in a plum-colored suit that might just have arrived from a London tailor.

Henry instantly recognized the man who followed. Who didn't know Sam Adams? There he was, with his massive head and towering forehead, looking as if he had slept in his clothes and wearing the same old rumpled wig.

Sam Sprague pointed out others among the leaders whom Henry had heard of but did not know by sight. Among them were Will Molineux, the fiery Irishman; Paul Revere, the silversmith whose shop was in North Square; handsome Dr. Joseph Warren.

John Hancock had gone into the pulpit. Just below him, facing the audience, some of the other leaders sat in high-backed chairs. Hancock held up his hand. "I declare this meeting in session," he said.

There were cries of "Where's Rotch?"

As everyone in Boston did by this time, Henry Purkitt knew that Francis Rotch was one of the tea consignees and the owner of the "Dartmouth."

"We sent him to the governor to get permission for

the tea ships to leave Boston," Hancock replied. "Samuel Adams will address you while we wait."

As Mr. Adams began to talk, Henry Purkitt thought back to the day he had wandered into a shipyard at dinnertime while on an errand for his master. Mr. Adams had been there talking to some of the hands. It had been the same way then as it was now; he didn't seem to be making a speech, and everything he said sounded mighty reasonable and right.

Sam Adams did not mention the tea at all. Right now he was telling the people a story:

"A Grecian philosopher, who was lying asleep upon the grass, was aroused by the bite of some animal upon the palm of his hand," he began. "He closed his hand suddenly as he awoke and found that he had caught a field mouse. As he was examining the little animal who dared attack him, it unexpectedly bit him a second time; he dropped it, and it made its escape. Now, fellow citizens, what think you was the reflection he made upon this trifling circumstance? It was this— *that there is no animal, however weak and contemptible, which cannot defend its liberty if it will fight for it.*"

There was not a sound in the Old South while the patriot spoke. The people listened, spellbound, and when he sat down they gave him an ovation.

Other speakers followed. Some urged caution, but the crowd was in no mood to accept such advice. Hoots and catcalls resounded in the church. Samuel Adams had planted something in the minds of his listeners.

John Hancock went back into the pulpit. He put a question to a vote: "Shall the tea be landed?"

There was a tremendous shout: "No!"

A reddish glimmer of light falling through the west windows of the Old South caught Henry Purkitt's eye. It was near sunset, and the rain had stopped.

Down on the main floor someone yelled, "A mob! A mob!" In the gallery an ear-shattering whistle startled Henry. Instinctively he glanced over at the puckish face of George Robert Twelves Hewes, who still had two fingers in his mouth. John Hancock rapped and called for order until the hubbub died down.

It was nearly six o'clock when Francis Rotch came in. He had a tormented look as he shouldered his way to the pulpit and talked for a moment with John Hancock. Then he faced the audience. "Governor Hutchinson refuses permission for the tea ships to leave Boston," he announced.

A great commotion of angry voices resounded throughout the church until John Hancock held up his hand and put a question to Francis Rotch: "Will you send your vessel back with the tea in her?"

Rotch threw up his hands. "I cannot do it, sir! It would prove my ruin!"

Henry Purkitt, crouched on the edge of his seat, held his breath. Down below, the massed audience sat rigid and silent, waiting. In the candlelight their faces seemed hewn from granite.

Samuel Adams was mounting to the pulpit. Save for the tremor in his voice that excitement always made worse, he might have been talking to his own family around the dinner table. "This meeting," he said, "can do nothing more to save the country."

Thinking of it afterward, Henry was sure that those words had been a signal, for no sooner were they out of Adams' mouth than the door of the Old South burst open and a wild shriek filled the air.

Young Purkitt's bulging eyes saw men with painted faces and feathers in their hair looming in the doorway. He seized Sam Sprague's arm. "Look!" he cried. "Indians! It's the war whoop!" Then he realized that the men were white.

Sam was already starting for the aisle. "Come on!" he yelled.

There was pandemonium on the lower floor when the two boys reached it. Men were shouting hoarsely: "Tea party! Tea party!" . . . "Boston harbor a teapot tonight!" . . . "Follow the Mohawks!" . . . "To Griffin's Wharf!"

Henry glanced back at Samuel Adams and John Hancock, standing together in front of the pulpit. Neither of them made any move to leave the church. There was an unmistakable look of triumph on Mr. Adams' face.

Outside, it was clear and colder, with a moon riding high in the sky. People were looking up and down in a confused way.

Then Henry Purkitt pointed toward Milk Street. "There they go!" he cried. The last of the Mohawks, brandishing hatchets, were just turning the corner.

Both apprentices took off after them. The rest of the crowd followed down the slope toward the harbor.

Henry shivered as he and his companion reached the footpath that led to Griffin's Wharf. The wind off the water had a sharp bite to it, and it drove dark clouds across the silver face of the moon. The three tea ships had been ordered into port, and now their great hulls cast black, lurking shadows, and their masts and spars, touched by the moonlight, were like bony skeletons of upraised arms.

The scene was strange, unreal. Usually, when the mob was out, there were screeches, whistles, and yells. But now the only sound was the steady, purposeful tramp of many feet heading for the wharf.

Henry and Sam approached it with the party disguised as Indians. Just ahead there was a low-voiced challenge and reply. On the wharf Henry could see several men with muskets. A man left the Mohawks' ranks and went up to one of them. "If you see any Tories 'round the wharf, chase 'em off," he ordered.

The guard raised his gun in salute. "Aye, Cap'n Pitts."

Pitts wore no disguise, but he seemed to be in command of the Mohawks. At a word from him they separated into three groups. Henry and Sam moved off in the wake of the one headed by Pitts.

Pitts said softly, "We've got the 'Beaver,' boys."

He led his detachment toward one of the vessels, a brig. Ahead of Henry a dwarfish figure scurried along— George Robert Twelves Hewes. The men clambered over the side and halted on the deserted foredeck. There was not a light visible nor any sign of life. Pitts glanced around the deck, then crooked a finger at Henry Purkitt.

"Go aft and see if you can find the mate," he directed. "We'll want the keys to the hold and a few lights. Tell him if there's no trouble made there'll be no damage done to the vessel."

Since he was a cooper's apprentice and often went aboard ships to repair casks and barrels, Henry had no difficulty in finding his way below deck.

"What's going on up there?" the ship's officer demanded.

Henry gave him Pitts' message.

After standing there uncertainly for a moment, the mate shrugged his shoulders. "I don't want any trouble." From his pocket he drew a huge, jingling bunch of keys and handed them to Henry. "I'll send the bosun up with the lanterns."

Up on deck Pitts had begun directing the preparations. He nodded in satisfaction as Henry gave him the keys and told him about the lights. Then he beckoned to George Robert Twelves Hewes.

"That whistle of yours working, George?"

For answer, Hewes inserted two fingers in his mouth and produced a piercing blast.

"I see it is," said Pitts dryly. "Suppose you act as our bosun, George. I don't know but what you ought to keep the whistle down a mite though. We don't want to wake the dead up in the Granary Burying Ground—

126

nor the watch on the men-o'-war just below us in the harbor."

Some of the men lit torches. The flares illuminated the motley crowd—the paint-daubed Mohawks, most of them wearing blankets over their shoulders, and the others garbed in working clothes with leather aprons and dilapidated three-cornered hats. Their faces had been smeared with soot, charcoal, grease, and whatever else had come to hand. Others were still coming aboard; Henry thought there must be fifty men on the "Beaver's" foredeck now.

"Open up that hold, some of you, and jump down there," Pitts ordered. "Those in the hold'll pass the chests forward and we'll hoist 'em up. The rest of you open 'em and dump the tea overside."

The men jumped to obey. Henry and Sam took a hand in getting off the hatch covers. A man near them grunted, "This ain't what the boys're used to. It's no more like it usually is when the mob's out than Sabbath meeting's like a husking bee!"

It certainly was orderly and peaceful. Everyone worked with quiet efficiency. The hoisting tackles began to creak and the big chests came swaying out of the hold. Those who had hatchets attacked them furiously as soon as they were lowered to the deck. The two boys grabbed one of the opened chests. It was heavy, and they had to wrestle hard with it, shifting it to the offshore rail of the "Beaver," but Henry felt a thrill as they heaved it up and dumped it over the side.

There was not a sound aboard the ship except for

the creaking blocks, the "scree-eack!" of ripped-open chests, the soft swish of the falling tea, and an occasional blast of George Robert Twelves Hewes' ever-ready whistle as he directed operations on deck. The air was heavy with the flowery perfume of the tea.

The two boys worked steadily, pausing only to catch their breaths. Once Henry heard the deep voice of the bell on King's Chapel striking eight o'clock. It might have been half an hour later when George Robert Twelves Hewes let go with a prodigious blast of his whistle and Pitts held up his hand.

"Ask the mate for brooms, some of you, and sweep the decks clean. The vessel's to be left just as she was. Those're the orders I've had. But not a grain of tea's to be left aboard—nor taken ashore, mind!"

The party fell to clearing the decks of the litter of spilled tea, splinters, and shreds of the canvas coverings of the chests. When all was shipshape aboard the "Beaver," the mate was sent for. "Pray look about you, sir," Pitts told him, "and see that your vessel's in order and no damage done."

The officer looked unhappy, but he looked around the deck and then nodded.

"Fall in on the wharf, fellows," Pitts ordered. "Then take off your shoes and empty 'em out."

As Henry and Sam stood shivering with the rest in their stocking feet, the men from the second brig, the "Eleanor," came ashore. By the time Pitts had made an inspection up and down the file of his men, those aboard the "Dartmouth" were finished, too.

Pitts' men led the rest of the Mohawks off the wharf. Those who had hatchets, pry-bars, and other gear shouldered them like muskets. In the moonlight Henry saw a great mass of people gathered at the head of Griffin's Wharf. They fell back respectfully and opened a way as Pitts and his men approached. There was no sound from the crowd.

As the procession started back up the long slope toward the center of town, a window in a house flew up. A rheumy-eyed man with the face of a codfish poked his head out. His coat was barely visible; heavy with gold lace, it signified the uniform of an officer in His Majesty's Navy.

Someone behind Henry Purkitt breathed, "It's the admiral! It's old Montague himself!"

Henry gazed in awe at Admiral Montague, commander of the British warships that had recently sailed into the harbor. It was plain that he was not amused at what he saw, though he spoke jovially enough, "Well, boys, you've had a fine, pleasant evening for your Indian caper, haven't you? But mind, those who dance must pay the fiddler!"

"Oh never mind, squire!" Pitts shouted. "Just come out here, if you please, and we'll settle the bill in two minutes!"

The admiral slammed down the window. Those at the head of the column set up a shout that ran like a lighted fuse down the line as Pitts' reply to the admiral was passed along. From somewhere in the ranks came a shrill burst of music as someone began to play a fife.

The tune was the spirited march, "Yankee Doodle."

For Henry Purkitt it had been the most exciting night of his life. But he thought uneasily of what Admiral Montague had said. The fiddler was going to have to be paid, all right. What would the government in London do when it heard about the Boston Tea Party? And what would happen to Samuel Adams and the other leaders of the Liberty Boys?

Chapter 11

NOT ONLY HAD Boston brewed a large pot of tea, but it had cooked up a very hot stew for itself as well. And considering how long it took for news to be carried across the Atlantic Ocean to London, the town's punishment was swift and it was harsh.

The Boston Tea Party set England by the ears, the whole country roused to fury. Did this treasonable lot of upstarts think they could spit in the King's eye and get away with it? They'd find out soon enough. Formerly, America had had many friends in Britain. Now scarcely one was left.

People wrote outraged letters to the London newspapers. "It will be best," said one, "to blow the town of Boston about the ears of its inhabitants." "A nest of rebels and hypocrites," another declared. Said a third, "Boston has proved itself to be a canker worm in the heart of America." "Hang about one hundred of these puritanical rebels!" demanded still another.

Lord North, the Prime Minister, was determined to make Boston wish it had swallowed its pride and the East India Company's tea together. The King, equally incensed, said, "We must master them," and once George III took hold of an idea he was like a bulldog and never let go.

As for Parliament, it lost no time in striking hard at Boston. First it passed the Boston Port Bill. The colonial port was to be closed as tight as the shell of a balky clam. Boston, which depended for its very life upon the shipping trade, was to be starved into submission. The Port Bill was passed by an overwhelming majority. Even America's great friend, Colonel Barré, who had called the Americans sons of liberty, voted for it.

Then England recalled Thomas Hutchinson as governor. Someone had to take the blame, and Hutchinson was a convenient scapegoat. He had been indiscreet enough to write those letters, which had turned the people of Boston against him. But for that, everything would have been all right, the Crown officials said. The people would have bought the cheaper tea, no matter what that rabble-rouser Adams tried to do about it.

What Boston needed was the hard fist of a military man to make it behave, a general with a military force behind him to see that his commands were obeyed. The Crown appointed General Thomas Gage as royal governor, with five regiments to be placed under his command. And these regiments were not going to be Sam Adams'. They would stay in Boston, not at Castle Island.

Nor was that all. Parliament, determined to force the people into obedience, changed the charter of Massachusetts Bay. Until then the House of Representatives, elected by the people, had been the most powerful section of the General Court. Now it was stripped of most of its authority. As for the Council, or upper house, it had always been chosen by the representatives, although the governor could turn down anyone he did not like. Under the new ruling the Council was to be selected by the Crown.

All judges were to be appointed by the governor, who could also remove them from office. Even trial juries, instead of being drawn from among the people, were to be picked by the sheriffs, who were also Crown appointees. Only the governor could call a town meeting, and he decided what subjects would be discussed at it.

Prior to the Tea Party, not all the patriot leaders had agreed with Samuel Adams that England was trying to take away the people's rights. But now there could be no question about it; England had taken away liberties enjoyed by all subjects of the King.

Parliament took one final slap at Boston by decreeing that henceforth Salem should be the capital of Massachusetts Bay.

As for Samuel Adams and other patriot leaders, they were not forgotten. Parliament passed a bill providing that "all disturbers of the King's peace" would be sent to England for trial.

Patriot leaders were alarmed at the new law. "It's aimed right at Sam Adams," they said. "If he's seized and taken to England, he'll surely hang."

In the British Coffee House and other Tory haunts

in Boston, heads nodded smugly when someone quipped, "Sam Adams shudders at the sight of hemp."

He did nothing of the kind. His friends were worried about him, but such threats never disturbed Sam. He went right on as if nothing had happened. And he had more to do than ever before. Not only did the cause demand every possible moment of his time, but he had a new job. With John Hancock and two other men he was named a fire warden for Boston. It was considered an important job, for ever since a terrible fire had almost wiped out Boston's business section in 1711, the town had dreaded another such disaster.

The job paid no salary, but of course that did not worry Sam. He got along. In fact, he seemed to be doing a little better about this time. John Adams, after visiting the family in the old house on Purchase Street in 1772, remarked in his diary that Cousin Sam had recently refinished and painted the outside, put new glass in the windows, repainted and papered it inside, and bought new furniture. Young Samuel Jr. had finished at Harvard and was practicing medicine in Boston.

How Samuel Adams managed to support himself and his family at all was a mystery to most people. For one thing, he apparently sold part of the property on which his house stood. And it is said that when Sam's debts became too mountainous, John Hancock would pay the bills or the Sons of Liberty would take up a collection.

One thing did cause Sam Adams some concern, however. All that had been gained for the cause by the

Boston Tea Party might still be lost. In London the government leaders stipulated that if Boston would pay the East India Company for the tea, Parliament would repeal the Port Bill. Benjamin Franklin, who had been shocked by the Tea Party, advised doing so in a letter to Thomas Cushing, Samuel Adams, John Hancock, and William Phillips, who were Boston's members of the House of Representatives.

Sam need not have worried. Two days after the news of the Port Bill reached Boston, he presided over a meeting at Faneuil Hall. When the suggestion was made to the people that they could avoid the worst part of their punishment if they paid for the tea, they shouted it down. That was the last time anyone in Boston heard about paying the fiddler, as Admiral Montague had put it.

The other American colonies were just as determined not to allow tea to be landed from ships that were arriving at ports all the way from New York to the Carolinas. In New York another consignment of tea was dumped into the harbor. At Greenwich, New Jersey, more Indians with white skins burned a tea cargo. In Annapolis, Maryland, the mob was not satisfied to destroy the tea; they burned the ship, too.

Letters approving the Tea Party and offers of support flooded in. The patriot Christopher Gadsden shipped rice given by Carolina planters to feed the people of Boston and wrote, "Don't pay for an ounce of the tea!" Colonel George Washington told Virginia's lawmakers, the House of Burgesses, "If need be I will raise one thousand men, subsist them at my own expense, and march myself at their head to the relief of Boston."

And Boston itself was determined never to yield. If the people could not drink the tea they were so fond of, they would find a substitute. Some took to drinking coffee. Ladies picked the leaves of a shrub called Labrador tea and brewed them, calling the horrible stuff Liberty Tea, smacking their lips bravely over it, and saying it was really quite good. "The tax on English tea gives it a far worse taste than this," they declared.

The first day of June, 1774, came, the day the port of Boston was to be closed. After that no tall, white-sailed ships arrived from far places and departed again, nor did fishing vessels come and go. Not even a garbage scow moved in the harbor. Much of Boston's food came from farms to the north and was transported across the Charles River from Charlestown. Even this source of supply was shut off.

The people who suffered first were the sailors, shipyard workers, and ropewalk hands. All along the shore, ships lay moored to the wharves. Their rotting lines gave out a dismal creaking as the vessels stirred drowsily with the tide. Anchors and chain cables grew red with rust. Green mildew spotted the ships' furled sails; barnacles fouled their hulls.

A Sabbath-like quiet hung over the waterfront. Little knots of sailors and men in working clothes stood about aimlessly on the street corners or lounged on the wharves, staring out at the deserted harbor. No busy sounds of saws and adzes came from the shipyards' empty stocks, bleaching in the sun, no tap-tap of chipping hammers on anchor cables, for there was need for neither new ships nor repairs on old ones. With no call for the thousands of ropes used in their rigging, the ropewalks were closed. In the summer heat, grass pushed six inches high between the cobblestones of the waterfront streets where once wagons and drays had steadily rolled.

Then the thing began to spread, like an epidemic of smallpox. Soon the merchants who depended upon ship cargoes for their trade had little to sell. And because the clerks and apprentices in the merchants' countinghouses had nothing to do, they were discharged. That meant they had no money to buy food. Soon neither they nor the grocers and bakers could buy leather from the tanners, shoes from the cordwainers, medicine from apothecaries. No one was building houses or repairing them. That put housewrights and bricklayers out of work. And so it went.

Before long, except for Boston's richest men, almost the only ones in town who had any money were the scarlet-coated soldiers of General Gage's army and the sailors from the men-of-war and transports in the harbor.

For now the troops had come. With drums thundering and fifes squealing an appropriate tune for Boston called "The World Turned Upside Down," the regiments tramped up King Street. Only two arrived at first, in mid June, the Fourth and the Forty-third. But more kept coming until there were five thousand soldiers in Boston by the end of October.

That made almost one soldier to every three inhabitants, most of them infantrymen, seasoned veterans of Europe's wars. But there were artillerymen, too, and fusiliers, and grenadiers wearing outlandish, high-peaked caps that made them look as if they had stepped out of the pages of some fairy tale.

Along King Street, the people watched as they came. Pretty daughters of Tories and Crown officials, demure in summery gowns of flowered dimity, with curls tucked under their gauze mob caps whose strings were tied fetchingly under their chins, sighed admiringly after handsome young officers. Boston would be gay that winter, they whispered to each other. Some even dared cry, "Huzza! Huzza for the King's Own!" as the Fourth Regiment swung by. The rest of the people watched in silence, but there was black hatred in their eyes.

Samuel Adams must have been very proud of his people. He no longer had to fear that they would yield. He had heard their answer when the question of paying for the tea was raised. And when General Gage offered work to housewrights and other workmen to put up barracks as winter quarters for the soldiers, they scorned it. Only Tories would take such work, and few of them dared do so.

Sam felt sure now that the great objective of his life would be achieved. All the patriots of Massachusetts Bay were squarely behind him, and there were many of them, Hancock, Josiah Quincy, Jr., Dr. Warren, Paul Revere, James Bowdoin, Robert Treat Paine, Joseph Hawley, and a host of others. His cousin John Adams was taking an active part in the events that were sweeping America toward revolution. Sam's good friend Tom Cushing, the speaker of the House of Representatives, was also active. Only James Otis was missing, his mind still too affected for him to be of use.

Not only the Massachusetts Bay patriots were with Samuel Adams. The aftermath of the Tea Party had shown that from New England to the Carolinas the people of America were aroused against the Crown.

One more thing was yet needed, Sam felt. His Committees of Correspondence had accomplished wonders, but writing letters to people is not as satisfactory as talking to them. So Samuel Adams set about to make his second great idea a reality.

On June 7, 1774, the General Court convened in Salem, the new capital. That day a rumor swept Salem like a fire through a tinder-dry forest. "Have you heard the news?" people demanded of each other excitedly. "They say Sam Adams and John Hancock've been arrested for treason! They're to be shipped to England to stand trial for their lives!"

As the hour for convening the House of Representatives approached and Sam Adams had not appeared, the Tory members grew jubilant. Some asked sneeringly of patriots, "Where is your leader?"

But Sam had not been arrested, only delayed. He arrived, and at the session he was appointed chairman of a committee of nine members to prepare a report to the governor on the state of the province.

All the members were patriots. Something about that fact aroused the Tories' suspicions that, just as they had feared, Samuel Adams had something new up his sleeve.

Sam did. But until it was accomplished it must at all costs be prevented from reaching General Gage's ears. Otherwise the governor could use his legal power to dismiss the House of Representatives.

Gage, too, was suspicious of what the patriots might do next. His military headquarters were still at Province House in Boston, but he had taken a summer home in Danvers, right next to Salem, so that he could keep a close watch on the representatives.

Reviewing the names of the other eight members of his committee, Samuel Adams hesitated over one. Leonard . . . Daniel Leonard . . . he claimed to be a patriot, but there were those who doubted it. Could he be a Tory spy . . . ?

Sam could take no chances. When the committee met, nothing but the most trivial matters were discussed. But afterward Sam called five trusted friends together secretly, outlined his plan, and convinced them it should be carried out.

When the same five met again with Samuel Adams the next night, each brought from among the members of the House a few friends he was sure he could trust. They, too, were persuaded that Sam's plan was a good one. The meetings were continued each night, a few more trusted representatives being added each time, until Sam had a majority of the votes of the House.

On June 17 they were ready. Although the patriots had induced most of the Tory members of the House to stay away because nothing important would be discussed that day, about a dozen of them appeared. Nevertheless, Speaker Thomas Cushing opened the session. Then Samuel Adams asked and was granted permission to put a motion before the House:

"That a General Congress of deputies meet in Philadelphia to consult together upon the present state of the colonies, and to deliberate and determine upon wise and proper measures for the recovery and establishment of their just rights and liberties, civil and religious."

That was Samuel Adams' second idea, a congress of all the colonies. Just as today we believe that the nations of the world can find ways to work together in unity for the good of all by meeting in the United Nations, so Adams saw that only by meeting together could the colonies unite and act together.

A gasp went up from the Tories as Sam finished reading his motion. This was treason! The governor must be notified at once. He must prorogue the House before the motion could be put to a vote. The Tories looked toward the doors. At each one stood a patriot guard, placed there by Adams. They did not have to try the doors to know they were locked.

A Tory rose and lurched toward the door, holding his hands over his stomach. "I am ill!" he groaned to the guard. "I am going to be sick!" The patriot had to let him through.

There was nothing sickly about the way the man leaped into his saddle the moment he got outside and galloped madly toward Danvers. When Gage learned what was going on, he acted swiftly. Seizing a quill, he dashed off a proclamation proroguing the House of Representatives.

"Take this to Salem," he ordered his secretary, Thomas Flucker. "Tell them the House of Representatives is prorogued. The members are to return to their homes."

Flucker hurried to Salem. Finding the door of the assembly hall barred, he hammered on it. "Open, in the King's name!" he shouted. "I have an official message from His Excellency Governor Gage!"

"The door is locked," the guard on the other side replied.

"Where is the key?"

"In Mr. Samuel Adams' pocket."

Fuming and raging, Flucker read the governor's proclamation to a crowd that had gathered outside the door. Then he went and read it to the Council. Both actions were rather silly since they did not the slightest good.

Meanwhile, inside the assembly chamber, Adams' motion, having been discussed, was put to a vote. It was passed, 120 to 12.

Samuel Adams, John Adams, Thomas Cushing, James Bowdoin, and Robert Treat Paine were appointed delegates to the congress. Every town in Massachusetts Bay was to share the expenses of the journey to Philadelphia by contributing five hundred pounds.

In Sam's blue eyes the future must have stood out sharp and clear now. Much work lay ahead for his pen and, in Philadelphia, for his persuasive tongue. But he knew that he would not stand alone at the congress. There would be others like him, men of stature in their own colonies who shared his views, men who could also write and speak convincingly and would have the respect and attention of the other delegates.

To Samuel Adams it was no longer a question of whether the American colonies would rise against the Crown, but only *when*. The proper time would come. In the meantime the people of Boston would tighten their belts and hold out.

Tighten their belts they did, but they did not starve. Although nothing moved in the harbor, there was plenty of traffic on the one road that led into the town. The peninsula on which Boston stood was connected to the mainland by a narrow strip of land called Boston Neck. Over the Neck road, carts and wagons rolled continually, bringing relief to Boston.

From the fishing village of Marblehead came ten tons of fish and a gift of money. Other Massachusetts Bay towns sent what food could be spared. From Connecticut came corn and rye; Maryland and Virginia sent meal, bread, and money. Carolina provided rice; Philadelphia sent money. And strangest of all, money arrived from London! Although most Englishmen had turned against Boston, the town still had a friend or two left in England, and prosperous ones at that.

As if Samuel Adams did not have enough to do these days, the provisions sent to Boston involved him in still another job. He was chairman of a committee to distribute the food among the needy and to buy more with the money that was sent.

Of all the gifts, the most heartening one came from the little wilderness settlement of Pomfret in northeastern Connecticut. About noon one blazing August day the bell of the Old Brick Church began to peal wildly. People poured out of their houses, heading first for the church and then streaming into Dock Square. In five minutes the square was choked with a milling crowd.

Suddenly someone shouted, "Stand back! Let 'em through!"

Near the Town Pump, where Cornhill led off in the direction of the Neck, the people fell back, opening a pathway. Much to everybody's amazement, a frightened, bawling flock of sheep burst out of Cornhill. The people craned their necks to see the man who was driving them, a barrel-chested farmer in homespun, striding along with a step that made it hard for those who recognized him to believe that he was nearly sixty years old.

The shouts were deafening. A man yelled, "It's Old Put! Huzza!"

"Who's Old Put?" an apprentice in the crowd bellowed into his companion's ear.

"Durned if I know," the other one replied.

An old man in front of them turned and glared. "Mean to say ye don't know old Put?" he screeched. "Ye ought to be ashamed! That's Colonel Israel Putnam. Druv that flock afoot, seventy mile, all the way from Connecticut in this heat, so's ye'll have enough to eat! He fought in the French War. There's no better scout in America than Old Put. Aye, and he'll be back a-fighting lobsterbacks this time, if they mean to have a war!"

He swept off his rusty three-cornered hat and waved it. "Hey, Put! Remember me? I was with ye at Fort Edward in 'fifty-seven. Be with ye this time if ye say so!"

Dock Square was a bedlam. Hats were sent sailing into the air; people cheered and laughed and nudged one another. Miraculously, a path opened straight through to the marketplace for the careering sheep, over a hundred of them.

Colonel Putnam acknowledged the cheers by taking off his hat and waving it. Under dark hair that had scarcely any gray in it, sweat rolled down his forehead onto an oddly boyish face that was as round and ruddy as a rising full moon. Light blue eyes swept the crowd, seeming to miss nothing. His walk was the effortless tread of the woodsman, as though his feet were padded.

Someone shouted, "Hey, Put! Come to get yourself a lobster?"

Putnam broke into a shy grin, looking pleased as a boy who has outdone himself in some feat of strength.

145

"Wal, I dunno," he drawled. "I see a few of 'em as I come along. Didn't look to me as if they're worth wasting a charge of powder on."

This reply set the crowd crazy with delight. The old man turned and glared again at the two young apprentices behind him.

"Aye," he said, "if ye were soldiers in a tight spot ye'd be almighty glad if Old Put was a-leading ye, young fellers. He'd get ye out of it, if anyone could. And he's not afraid of aught that walks on two legs, or four, either!"

No, Samuel Adams did not have to worry that the people of America would back down now. Not while there were fearless men like Israel Putnam. Nor would the people of Boston back down while Sam was away in Philadelphia. They would stand like rocks while Britain tried to starve them out.

ꙮ Chapter 12 ꙮ

Now rumors flew thick and fast in Massachusetts Bay that Samuel Adams was to be arrested for treason and sent to England to be tried for his life. A number of friends warned him to be careful.

James Warren, the patriot of Plymouth, wrote Sam: " 'Beware the Ides of March' was a caution given to Caesar, and his neglect of it was afterward regretted by his friends. His rid the world of a tyrant; and yours may deprive your country of the wisdom and virtue of a distinguished patriot."

From his home in Northampton, Joseph Hawley wrote to John Adams: "Pray, sir, let Mr. Samuel Adams know that our top Tories here give out most confidently that he will certainly be taken up before the Congress."

Samuel Adams refused to be frightened. Probably he felt sure that General Gage had no intention of seizing him at that time.

Gage, a shrewd and cautious man, was determined to do nothing that would start a war if he could help it. He was trying hard to be as fair to the people as possible and to see that his soldiers behaved themselves. He liked Americans. In fact, he had married one, beautiful Margaret Kemble of New Jersey. And as an officer of His Majesty's Army he had spent more than twenty years in America.

Gage would have liked nothing better than to ship Sam Adams to England and be rid of him and his troublemaking, but the patriot was a thorny problem, being more popular in Boston than he had ever been. Gage knew if he arrested Sam now the people would rise in fury.

So he tried another way to silence Sam. Some of the patriots could be bought. One of the most trusted of them, Dr. Benjamin Church, was already in the pay of the British. Perhaps Sam Adams could be tempted.

If so, the time to do it was now. When Gage prorogued the House of Representatives, Adams' salary as clerk of the House ended. His money troubles were going to be more acute than ever.

There are no official documents or records to prove that Gage did try to bribe Samuel Adams, but so many people wrote and spoke of it afterward that it seems plain that something of the sort happened.

Sam's daughter Hannah said in later years, when she was sixty-two years old, that Gage sent a colonel in command of one of the British regiments to the house on Purchase Street to make an offer. Her father, she declared, listened politely to the governor's messenger, then rose to his feet, his eyes blazing. "Sir," he said in a voice that quavered even more than usual, "no personal consideration shall ever induce me to abandon the righteous cause of my country. Tell Governor Gage it is the advice of Samuel Adams to him no longer to insult the feelings of an exasperated people!"

Some years after the Revolution one of Adams' biographers asked him about it. All Sam replied was, "A guinea never glistened in my eyes," apparently meaning that he had not been tempted. And several persons claimed that they knew a bribe had been offered.

How much was Gage willing to pay? After Samuel Adams' death, John Avery, the executor of his estate, said he found papers proving that Sam and his son were each to be given a thousand pounds a year for life. That was a great deal of money in those days. It would have made them both well-to-do.

Whatever happened, we may be sure of one thing; if General Gage thought Samuel Adams would turn traitor for money or anything else, he knew very little about the character of the man he was dealing with. Time after time Sam proved that money meant nothing to him. True, he never forgot the fact that the Hutch-inson family helped to bring about the Land Bank failure that ruined his father. But it was not the money that concerned him; it was the injury and injustice of the deed that Sam was never able to forgive.

As for deserting the patriots for any reason, it is impossible to conceive of the idea. As we have seen, from the moment he first became interested in politics, nothing else mattered. Anyone who underestimated or misjudged Sam Adams sooner or later had to admit the error . . . and sometimes learned that he was as formidable an enemy as he was a powerful ally.

The time for the Continental Congress, as it was called, to meet in Philadelphia was now approaching. It was a high point in Sam Adams' political career, as well as a great event in his personal life; this was to be the longest journey he had ever made. He had never before traveled more than a few miles into the countryside from Boston.

A flurry of excitement in the Adams household must have preceded his departure. Besides making all the preparations for the trip, Sam was concerned about leaving his family. How would they get along without his small salary as clerk of the House? What if armed rebellion broke out during his absence . . . might not the family of the Chief Incendiary be the first to suffer at the hands of the British soldiers? His cousin John Adams was taking the precaution of moving his family back to Braintree.

But Sam's son was living at home, and his medical practice earned him an income. Dr. Samuel would see that the family got along. And there was Betsy, standing as firm as a rock against trouble. She would manage.

Betsy Adams, of course, was worried about her husband's wardrobe. The other delegates, prosperous men, had no such problems; but what would Sam wear? The disreputable old brown suit? Betsy's heart must have sunk as she thought of it. He would be meeting distinguished men from the other colonies, many of them wealthy, and it was important for him to look well. But there was no money to buy new clothes.

Undoubtedly Betsy was still wrestling with the problem one night in July when there was a knock at the door. Sam got up and opened it. A man he did not know stood there.

"I am a tailor, Mr. Adams," the caller said. "May I take your measurements, sir?"

Samuel Adams' mouth fell open. Perhaps he was thinking of General Gage's hopes of bribing him. "Who sent you here?" he demanded.

"Some of your patriot friends," the tailor replied. "I was asked not to reveal their names, but they instructed me to measure you for a suit."

"It is very good of them, but I cannot . . ." Sam began.

Betsy Adams interrupted him, "Oh Sam . . . !" Her voice was pleading. Both she and Hannah had risen and advanced to the door.

"You are going to Philadelphia to represent Massachusetts Bay, Sam," his wife went on. "You must look your best. Your true and generous friends have thought of that, I am sure. This is no time for pride!"

What could Sam do? He let the man come in and stood quietly while his measurements were taken. Then the tailor bowed politely and left.

A few minutes later there was another knock. This time it was a hatter. He was followed by a shoemaker and by other tradesmen. By then Sam was too bewildered and overcome to do more than show them in and submit obediently to their requests.

On the morning of August 10, 1774, the delegates to the Continental Congress met at Tom Cushing's mansion on Beacon Hill. Their wives, and John Hancock, Josiah Quincy, Jr., and other patriot leaders and Sons of Liberty were there to see them off. There were only four delegates, since James Bowdoin's wife was ill and he had had to give up the journey.

Samuel Adams was the last to arrive. Outside, a crowd that had collected cheered as he and Betsy Adams came up the street. When the two entered the house, those who were gathered there gasped in astonishment, even though they were already prepared for the sight of Sam in his new finery.

And what a sight he was! His claret-colored suit of fine broadcloth had white buttons bearing the Liberty Cap emblem of the Sons of Liberty. Above white silk stockings there were gold buckles at his knees, silver ones on his shining new shoes, lace at his wrists and throat. A glossy new wig bushed out from under his elegant cocked hat. And in his hand he swung a gold-headed cane.

Sam actually strutted as he went up to the door of Tom Cushing's home. Who could blame him? Even a man who cares not a whit about clothes and treats them shamefully can be a little excited over a handsome new wardrobe. Besides, there was something more than human vanity that made him strut. It was the pride and pleasure that shone in Betsy Adams' eyes.

Tom Cushing's elegant coach, drawn by four horses, pulled up now at the door. Beside the driver sat a groom, with two footmen in livery perched behind, while four mounted and armed men rode alongside. All were servants of John Hancock.

The four delegates entered the vehicle, richly upholstered inside in crimson silk, and drove off.

Standing in the doorway, Betsy Adams waved, fighting to keep back the tears as she watched her beloved husband leave. Better that anyone else, she knew that his clothes would not look the same when he reached Philadelphia. But they would still be new. Massachusetts Bay would not have cause to be ashamed of its most distinguished patriot, the man who had never given up the fight for liberty—Samuel Adams, delegate to the First Continental Congress.

The new clothes certainly were somewhat rumpled at the end of the long and strenuous journey, but Sam Adams never gave them another thought. There was work to be done.

Work he did, though there is little in the records of the Continental Congress to show it. All through the sessions Sam and the other Massachusetts Bay delegates played a very cautious and retiring part. They had realized beforehand that, unless they did so, the Congress would fail. There was jealousy of Massachusetts Bay among the other colonies. Some feared that the New England province wanted to rule them all. Others believed that Massachusetts was determined to start a war with England. There was also considerable fear among the Episcopalians, Quakers, Presbyterians, and Anabaptists present, of the stern and bigoted puritanism of New England's Congregationalists.

The Continental Congress met for the first time in Carpenter's Hall on September 5, 1774. It started off smoothly enough with the election of Peyton Randolph of Virginia as chairman, and Charles Thomson of Pennsylvania as secretary. The Massachusetts Bay delegates made no attempt to gain either of these posts.

There was a sensation that afternoon, however, when a discussion began over the method of voting. Some delegates wanted each of the twelve colonies represented (Georgia had failed to attend) to have one vote. Others favored one for each of the fifty-six delegates, which would have given some of the colonies more votes than others.

Patrick Henry of Virginia rose, a lean, dark, blue-eyed man whose fiery oratory had already made him famous. Now he cried, "Let freemen be represented by numbers alone! The distinctions between Virginians, Pennsylvanians, New Yorkers, New Englanders are no more. I am not a Virginian but an American!"

All through the sessions of the Continental Congress, Samuel Adams' expression was never to give any hint of what he was thinking, and it did not now. But Patrick Henry's words must have made Sam glow inside. An American! Surely Sam Adams felt drawn to this man whose unpowdered wig was also uncombed and whose suit was almost as carelessly kept as the one Sam himself wore at home in Boston.

There were other delegates whose views on liberty

were nearly as strong as Samuel Adams'—Richard Henry Lee and Colonel George Washington of Virginia, Christopher Gadsden of South Carolina, Roger Sherman of Connecticut, and Governor Stephen Hopkins of Rhode Island. But most of them were more conservative. Sam Adams was sure that at least one of them, Joseph Galloway of Pennsylvania, was a Tory. He was right about that. All through the sessions Galloway made it clear that he advocated British sovereignty, despite all the problems it created for the colonies. No doubt there were others who felt the same way, but Galloway never gained a strong following in the Congress.

Trouble started brewing over a petty religious matter on the second day. As the session opened, Tom Cushing rose to say that because the situation which had brought the Congress together was so serious, he felt the meeting should be opened with a prayer by Mr. Duché, a minister. John Jay of New York got up and said he was against it. There could be no minister who would suit everybody.

Some of the delegates were already bristling. Then Samuel Adams came forward.

"I hope I am no bigot," he said, speaking very quietly, "for I can hear a prayer from a gentleman who is a friend to his country. I am a stranger in Philadelphia, but I have heard that Mr. Duché deserves that character."

Mr. Duché was a Church of England minister. The delegates stared at each other. Could this be Samuel

Adams, the Congregationalist who was often called "the Last of the Puritans," making such a suggestion? Sam won them over by his attitude of tolerance. There was no further objection to the prayer or to Mr. Duché. And then an electrifying piece of news arrived, almost like a warning that this First Continental Congress *must* work together.

On that very day a report reached Philadelphia that General Gage had seized some powder the patriots had stored in Charlestown. Massachusetts Bay and Connecticut had taken arms, the story ran. Twenty thousand militia were marching on Boston. The town had been bombarded and set afire by a British fleet.

Carpenter's Hall saw no more of the thunderstruck delegates that day, for they immediately adjourned and hurried out to learn more details. It was two days before a messenger from Boston brought the news that the report was false.

Samuel Adams had not expected the First Continental Congress to accomplish a great deal. It was enough that it had been assembled for mutual discussion. Later, at a second one, more might be done. But the Powder Alarm, as it was called, was an object lesson to the delegates. Such a thing, they saw, could really happen. It would be just as well if they showed England that they meant business.

Joseph Galloway suspected Samuel Adams of having plotted the Powder Alarm for that very reason. It is almost certain he did not, but it may well have spurred the Continental Congress to go along with more of Sam's ideas than he had dreamed possible.

When a swift rider was needed to carry dispatches from the Sons of Liberty or the Committee of Correspondence in Boston to those organizations in other colonies, Paul Revere was one of the men to deliver them. He made a number of such journeys in the years before the Revolution, and now he arrived in Philadelphia bringing a document known as the "Suffolk Resolves."

Boston was located in Suffolk County, as were a number of the larger Massachusetts Bay towns surrounding it. These towns had held a convention and passed resolutions, which were now read to the Congress. Dr. Joseph Warren had written them, and they were as strongly worded as anything that had ever come from the pen of Samuel Adams. A strong militia must be raised in every town and trained for war, they said. The Port Bill and the other punitive measures Parliament had enacted were to be disobeyed. In the future Massachusetts Bay should impose and collect its own taxes. And not only should nonimportation be resumed, but all trade with England, import and export, must be stopped.

It seemed impossible that the Continental Congress would approve such a revolutionary document. Samuel Adams must have been stunned, but overjoyed, when the delegates rose in their seats and broke into loud applause.

Joseph Galloway and James Duane of New York, another delegate who leaned strongly toward the Crown, were furious. "For Congress to countenance such a statement is tantamount to a complete declaration of war," Galloway said. Nevertheless, the Continental Congress voted to approve the Suffolk Resolves.

Then the Congress set to work in earnest. It adopted a Declaration of Rights setting forth the liberties to which the people of America, as British subjects, were entitled. Samuel and John Adams were members of the committee that drafted the declaration.

Next, and most important, the Congress adopted a document called the Continental Association. The chief clause in it was an agreement not to engage in trade of any kind with England. True, each of twelve colonies would have to approve it. And trade in rice and indigo, upon which South Carolina depended for its existence, was allowed to continue. Nevertheless, it was a powerful weapon against England, and it was what Samuel Adams wanted most of all to see adopted.

It was late in October now. Sam was anxious to return home. He and the other delegates had been royally entertained in Philadelphia; they had dined on turtle, baked oysters, creams, custards, and other delicacies. They had toasted each other with the finest Madeira wine. But Sam would rather have been surrounded by his family in the old house on Purchase Street, eating hasty pudding.

The First Continental Congress ended on October 26. Two days later the four Massachusetts Bay delegates climbed into Tom Cushing's coach once more, and it drove off, heading north. Philadelphia was gray and dismal that morning under a chill downpour. As the wheels of the coach clattered over the cobbles, Sam

Adams sank back into the soft cushions with a sigh of relief. It would be good to be back in Boston with his wife Betsy. He was tired, but very happy.

At the Congress he had met men whom he had previously known only by their signatures on letters. There had been squabbles, disagreements, problems, but the delegates had gotten to know one another. Best of all, they had found that they could straighten out their disputes by discussion. For the first time twelve of the thirteen American colonies stood united in the resolutions and agreements they had approved.

There was much more yet to be done, but the way ahead was clear now. Only a little longer. . . .

Chapter 13

IT WAS THIRTEEN days before Samuel Adams saw Boston once more. In New York, Robert Treat Paine left the delegates and took passage on a packet boat bound for Newport, Rhode Island. When the other three reached Cambridge, John Adams hired a horse and rode directly to his home in Braintree. Sam Adams and Tom Cushing continued on in the coach.

Boston Neck was a desolate place in summer. Crossing it late one bleak November afternoon, the two returning delegates must have found it even more dreary. There were few houses, and the one weather-beaten tavern along the road had a lonely, brooding look. In the distance, silhouetted against the sky, they could see the gallows on which Boston's criminals, and often enough a captured pirate, were executed. Beyond it, on the stocks of a shipyard along the marshy shore, the bare bones of a half-finished vessel, left to rot when the port was closed, might have been the carcass of a whale picked clean by the wheeling gulls. The tide was out, and a smell of dead clams on the mud flats hung over the land.

To its desolation was now added an ominous look. An ancient fort, which had been falling to pieces when the Philadelphia-bound coach had passed by in August, was no longer an abandoned shell. The crumbling walls had been repaired and strengthened. In place of the rusty, useless cannon, once mounted on the ramparts, new guns pointed toward Roxbury on the mainland. Adams and Cushing had heard that the fort was being restored. Nevertheless they leaned out and stared at what General Gage had done. Sam found satisfaction in the sight, for here was additional proof that England intended to maintain her strong hold on the colonies, by force if necessary.

A red coated sentry stepped out into the road and hailed the coach. After identifying the occupants he waved permission for it to continue. Ahead, in the gathering twilight, Sam caught sight of a gray jumble topped by church spires. The church bells rang out in joyful welcome as the coach entered the town, for the delegates' return was being awaited all over Boston.

Betsy Adams shed a few tears of happiness when Sam entered the door of their home, and the family reunion that followed was a warm, happy one. There was concern in Betsy's eyes, however, when she told her husband the latest news.

She spoke of the fortifications on the Neck. "It's not just that, Sam. They say General Gage has grown bolder in every way. Now there are rumors that the Parliament in London is going to take sterner measures against the people."

Did Sam know that the patriots had formed a Provincial Congress and had already met in Salem? Yes, and he had been elected a member, along with Hancock, Cushing, John Adams, Joseph Warren, and others.

He knew about that, but he had not heard Betsy's next piece of news. "The Provincial Congress appointed a Committee of Safety to buy twenty thousand pounds worth of arms and ammunition and to reorganize the militia. There are companies marching and drilling on all the greens of the villages outside Boston."

"And there's a special battalion in each regiment that's to hold itself in readiness to march at the shortest notice," Dr. Sam added.

"They call them the Minutemen," Hannah put in.

"Oh Sam," Betsy cried, "I worried about you all the time you were away, and now that you're home I'm worried even more for fear General Gage will have you seized!"

Sam reassured her, "Have no fear, my dear."

There was one other piece of news. Will Molineux had died in October of a stroke some said was brought on by his terrible fits of rage. Sam Adams reflected sadly that the rough, fiery-tempered Irishman had done his share of work for the cause. In any future action, the leaders would be officers commanding the militia. Perhaps he wondered what his role would be in the coming struggle. But he had no time to waste on such speculations as he plunged into the work that was waiting for him.

There was to be another meeting of the Provincial

Congress late in the month. The Donation Committee, of which Sam was chairman, was very busy handling the even greater flood of money and food that was still pouring into Boston. His pen was badly needed here to deny rumors circulated by the Tories that all the money went into the pockets of the committee.

Most important of all, Sam was a member of the Committee of Safety. There was urgent need for it to arrange for the distribution of guns, powder, bullets, and military equipment to some of the near-by towns, where it was to be hidden. This committee had to work in great secrecy, for General Gage's spies were watching every move they made. In spite of their precautions, one of their members, Dr. Benjamin Church, was selling the secrets to Gage, and his treason was not uncovered until after war actually broke out.

To ferret out what was going on in the towns outside Boston, Gage made use of the Tories who lived there and also used his own officers and soldiers. That winter of 1774-1775 started out as a cold one, but soon after the first of the year the weather moderated. From then on it was the mildest winter in the memory of the oldest inhabitant of Boston. Therefore, it was quite natural, on these pleasant, almost springlike days, for small groups of British officers to ride out into the countryside.

Even so, certain people wondered if their excursions were as innocent as they appeared. Paul Revere was one of the suspicious ones and became a member of a group that was formed to patrol Boston day and night.

They observed the movements of all British forces in the area and reported their information to the Committee of Safety.

And there was need for such precaution.

In Concord, twenty miles from Boston, a man in working clothes came into the shop of old Sam Barrett, a patriot gunsmith.

"My name's Wood," he said. "I'm a Liberty man. Do you know of any work for a gunsmith hereabouts?"

Mr. Barrett pricked up his ears, but he was cautious enough to take the stranger to the patriot leaders of Concord. They questioned Wood carefully, then, satisfied that he was a patriot, gave him a musket lock to repair in Sam Barrett's shop. He did an expert job on it.

Then they took him to a locked room in the town hall. When the door was opened, the gunsmith found himself looking into the grim muzzles of a dozen cannon stored there. Beside them, muskets were piled high. Farther back, flour barrels were stacked all the way to the ceiling.

Colonel James Barrett, commander of the Concord militia, picked up a musket. "Can you make guns like this one, Wood?"

"Aye, like this or any kind you want, sir. But I'll have to get my tools. I left 'em at the tavern in Lexington."

"All right," said Colonel Barrett, "go get 'em. We'll give you plenty of work."

So John Howe, not Wood, a gunsmith in His Majesty's Army, started out for Boston, not Lexington. Nor did the Concord patriots ever see him again.

Meanwhile, in London, America's old friend, William Pitt, now Lord Chatham, appealed to the House of Lords in Parliament to end Boston's punishment for the Tea Party. "There is no time to be lost!" he cried. "The very first drop of blood will make a wound that will not easily be skinned over. Repeal, therefore, my Lords, *repeal*, I say!"

No one paid any attention. Lord North wanted even more severe punishment. The king was doggedly determined to make America submit. Plans were made to increase the number of soldiers in Boston to twenty thousand, more than the town's whole population, and to station a British fleet in the harbor.

By now the reports that the patriot leaders were to be seized became even more persistent. A London newspaper said that Samuel Adams, John Hancock, and Benjamin Franklin were to be hanged. Letters received in Boston mentioned others as well, but all the accounts named Adams and Hancock.

In genuine alarm some of Sam's friends came to him. "You must leave Boston!" they pleaded. "We have information that a sloop has arrived from London bearing orders for General Gage to arrest you and John Hancock!"

Whether Sam became concerned at last, we do not know, but doubtless his family added their entreaties to leave. And since the Provincial Congress was then meeting in Cambridge, the Adamses moved to that neighboring town across the Charles River. There they stayed in the home of Betsy's father, the merchant Francis Wells.

The Provincial Congress ended its sessions in Cambridge on February 16, 1775, then met again on March 22, this time in Concord.

Before leaving for Concord, Samuel Adams said good-by to his family once more. He was one of five delegates to the Second Continental Congress, which was to meet in Philadelphia on May 10. Rather than journey back to Cambridge, he planned to leave directly from Concord.

John Hancock was also a delegate, and when the Provincial Congress adjourned in Concord early in April he said to Sam, "Since there is plenty of time, there is no need to start for Philadelphia immediately. You and I are invited to spend a few days at my cousin Mrs. Clark's in Lexington."

Sam gladly accepted, thinking to relax a little before setting out on the arduous journey. There would be comfort and good food at the home of the Reverend Jonas Clark, the Lexington minister. Plenty of good conversation, too, for there would be quite a gathering there. Another guest would be John Hancock's Aunt Lydia, widow of Uncle Thomas who had left him all his money and the house on Beacon Hill. She had driven out from Boston, bringing pert, pretty Dorothy Quincy with her. Sam knew there was another reason Hancock wanted to go to Lexington; John had been sparking Dolly Quincy for three years, but she still had not made up her mind about him. The opportunity to continue his courtship was too good to pass up, especially since he was going to be away in Philadelphia for a long spell.

It was pleasant in Lexington. The weather was springlike, and for the first time in many weeks Sam enjoyed the luxury of having nothing in particular to do. John probably found time to spend with the fetching Dolly and also stroll with Sam down to the village green, a quarter of a mile away, for a glass of flip in Buckman's Tavern and a friendly discussion of politics.

Around dinnertime on Sunday, April 16, however, after Mr. Clark had preached his morning sermon at the meetinghouse, the restful quiet of the parsonage was broken by a clatter of hoofs outside. Very likely the minister, a devout, sternfaced man, did not try to conceal a frown of displeasure at the ungodliness of the rider who dared to be abroad on the Sabbath.

John Hancock and Samuel Adams looked at each other and went outside. Dismounting in the yard was a stocky man with dark eyes and hair and a bluff, bold, squarish face. It was Paul Revere, courier for the patriots of Boston.

Revere spoke to Hancock, who was in the lead, "I have an urgent message for you and Mr. Adams from Dr. Warren, sir."

Hancock broke the seals of the letter hastily. "Warren says the Regulars are expected out," he muttered as he scanned the message. "They may be heading for Concord after the stores there. Warns us that we may be seized."

He turned to Revere, "I'll see that they're told in Concord to move the stores to a new hiding place and alert the Minutemen." With a nod the courier mounted again and rode off.

Neither patriot seems to have been alarmed by the news. They did not have to leave for several days yet, and since a squad of Lexington militiamen was assigned to guard the Clark home at night, the two felt no concern for their safety. They stayed on, enjoying the fine weather and the good company.

People went early to bed in the country; so as midnight approached on Tuesday, April 18, the household in the parsonage had been sound asleep for several hours. No one heard the furious thunder of hoofbeats outside.

Paul Revere, making his famous headlong gallop through the countryside under a high-riding moon, reined up in the dooryard and dismounted, shouting, "Open up there! Open the door!"

The sergeant in charge of the guard came hurrying up. "Quiet!" he demanded in a raucous whisper. "The ladies and gentlemen are all abed. Do not disturb them with any noise."

"Noise!" Revere bawled. "There'll be noise enough soon! The Regulars are out!" And he pounded loudly on the parsonage door.

The household was soon aroused, and Mr. Clark, holding a candle, came to the door. Not recognizing Revere at first, he was doubtful about letting him in, but close behind him, John Hancock called out, "Come in, Paul!"

The family crowded around the new arrival. Sleepy-eyed Samuel Adams looked like anything but the Chief Incendiary in his night rail and nightcap. In his, Mr. Clark bore no trace of the black-robed dignity of his pulpit. Aunt Lydia and Dorothy Quincy managed to look presentable, having thought to slip on cloaks, but the elegant John Hancock, in silk lounging robe and Moroccan slippers, put them all to shame.

Everyone listened, wide-eyed and speechless, as Paul Revere told them that a force of British soldiers was headed toward Lexington. Already they could hear the shouts and pounding footsteps of the Minutemen outside, running for the village green.

Hancock excused himself and left the room, returning a few minutes later fully dressed. As he began to buckle on his sword Adams asked, 'Where are you going, John?"

"To take my place with the Minutemen," Hancock replied.

A long harangue to stop him immediately started. Finally Sam put his arm around John's shoulders. "It is not our business," he pleaded. "We belong to the cabinet." Why he said "cabinet" instead of "Continental Congress" no one knows, but that was the way Dolly Quincy remembered it years later. Mr. Clark also added his entreaties that Hancock not endanger his life with the Minutemen. A second courier, William Dawes, rode in during the discussion; he and Paul Revere then galloped off to Concord.

For some time Hancock refused to listen to any plea or argument to keep him from leaving. He made a show of cleaning his gun; nevertheless he made no move to depart. Being a man of great personal vanity and ambition, perhaps he could not resist the chance to play the hero and patriot in front of Dolly and Sam. But at last he consented, reluctantly, to go with Adams to the greater safety of Woburn, a dozen miles away.

By then the night was almost over, and grayness was lightening the east as a chaise rolled up to the door of the parsonage. The two patriot leaders did not waste a moment in good-bys but climbed into the vehicle and drove off.

The Minutemen had been mustered on the green in Lexington, only to be dismissed but instructed to stand by. Most of them went into Buckman's Tavern until the roll of a drum brought them tumbling out again. They fell into ranks and waited, watching the dawn break over the village.

The sun rose upon a countryside radiant with the beauty that only an April morning can have. In the marshy places in the meadows, its rays made patches of cowslips shine like a scattered treasure of golden coins. Redwings, teetering on cattails, trilled praises of springtime. In the dank, wooded places, the early wild flowers peeped shyly through the carpet of dead leaves. A faroff thrush caroled his joyous song. In the orchards the apple buds, pink as a maiden's cheek, were nearly ready to burst forth. It was the kind of morning that tempted a schoolboy to leave his chores and go fishing. Under the overhanging banks of the brooks, the trout would be voraciously hungry.

But there would be no fishing for boys or men that day. For now, far down the road that led east toward Menotomy, the Lexington Minutemen could see what looked like a long scarlet ribbon lost off some giantess' cap, save that it was moving, moving toward them.

Closer . . . ever closer. Standing on the village green they watched the redcoats with shouldered muskets approach. In the morning haze the naked bayonets stuck up like a forest silver-tipped with frost. They could see the crazy, peaked caps of the grenadiers, too, and white-clad legs moving with practiced precision.

There were only about seventy militiamen on the green, farmers and farmers' boys in their everyday homespun and their rusty-looking cocked hats. How many well-trained and equipped soldiers they were facing they did not know, although someone who had ridden in said seven hundred. The sight of that oncoming red ribbon was enough to scare even seasoned fighting men. Scared the Minutemen were, but they stood fast.

Without warning it happened; a single musket shot rang out. Who fired it no one knew, and no one would ever know.

Then the village defenders saw the light infantry at the head of the British column halt and kneel. A brilliant flash of lightning seemed to leap from their gun muzzles, and the blast of its thunder echoed and re-echoed through the village of Lexington. A blue curtain of smoke rose up and billowed over the green.

When it lifted, a haze of blue-gold dust remained, shimmering in the pale, slanting rays of the sun.

Through it the wives and daughters of villagers, watching from their windows, saw the ragged line of farmers fall to pieces and run away, except for those who lay, not stirring.

Now the British infantry swept forward in a long undulating line, shouting like madmen. Their commander, Major Pitcairn, rode hard, mingling with them, cursing, striking up soldiers' muskets, trying to stop the firing he had not ordered.

In the middle of the green a homespun-clad figure dragged itself up from the trampled turf. The man tottered to his feet, fired, and sank to his knees. As he tried to reload, he toppled and lay still.

Over on the far side of the green, another Minuteman ran with desperate strides toward a house near Mr. Clark's barnlike church. The door of the dwelling swung open, and the frantic figure of a woman flung itself toward the running man. He crumpled, made a scrambling, crablike movement, got half to his knees, stretched his arms toward his wife, and died.

In the chaise, making its way toward Woburn, Sam Adams was so amiable and chipper that no one would have guessed that his night's sleep had been interrupted by the country's call to arms. Gazing out upon the sunlit beauty of the rolling meadows and woodland, he drew a deep breath and said to John Hancock, "What a glorious morning!"

Both men heard faintly in the distance behind them a low rumble of musket fire. In silence they gazed at each other significantly.

It would be late that night in Billerica, where they went after Woburn, before they would learn the whole story of that nineteenth of April, 1775. How, at Concord Bridge, the Minutemen stood fast and gave the British a volley that broke their ranks and sent them fleeing helter-skelter back toward Concord village, where other companies had found and were destroying a few of the hidden stores. And how, as the redcoats fell back toward Boston, they were harassed every step of the way by the farm-born and village-bred Minutemen who took up concealed positions behind stone walls along the road and fired their muskets at the British soldiery in a gallant defense of home and liberty.

Imagine a scene that afternoon. On a craggy hill a militia company lies hidden. Never having been under fire before, each man looks nervously to the priming of his musket as he waits. Suddenly one of them points in the direction of Concord.

"Here they come!" he rasps hoarsely.

Although the British are too far away for the patriot soldiers to realize it, they are not only coming but running, all but exhausted. Since noon they have been driven before a storm of bullets that seem to come from nowhere. In their ranks, men keep dropping; yet they are unable to return the fire of an enemy they cannot see, an enemy who does not fight by rules learned in Europe but who picks off his targets from behind every house, barn, wall, and clump of bushes.

The officer commanding the patriot company is an older man who fought in the French and Indian War.

He knows the importance of inspiring courage in his men by appearing unconcerned.

"Well, boys," he says calmly, "Sam's done it. If 'twasn't for Sam Adams, we'd all be King-lovers. Did it all by himself, too."

The men welcome the conversation, anything to keep their minds off the scarlet column that will soon pass by. There is a chorus of objections.

"I dunno 'bout that, now," says one. "There was plenty of others."

"Sam's the only one who never gave up," the officer retorts. "I know. Served with him in the House of Representatives, didn't I? When the rest of 'em wanted to make up with the Britainers, Sam kept right on a-hammering. Letters to the newspapers, speeches, caucuses with the shipyard hands. Knew more about that Tea Party than he let on, I'll warrant."

"How 'bout John Hancock?" one man asks.

"Hancock, you say? Why, he'd been a Tory ready to kiss His Pigheaded Majesty's foot if it hadn't been for Sam Adams. Sam showed him which side to butter his bread on! Good thing, too, with all that money in the Hancock countinghouse. You know what they say: 'Sam Adams writes the letters and John Hancock pays the postage.' "

"There was Otis though . . ." another man begins.

"Otis? Crazy as a coot most of the time. He did fine when he was in his right mind, but he's been no use to the Liberty Boys for a long time."

174

"They say John Adams did a lot," still another militiaman ventures.

"Aye," replies the officer, "that he did. But even he quit politics altogether for a spell. Only Sam kept a-going. You know what Stingy Tommy Hutchinson called him? The Chief Incendiary. Well, Sam's lit a fire under the Britainers now that Gage and his lobsterbacks won't put out in a hurry."

He squints down the road at the approaching British column. "Here they come, boys! Look at 'em run! It's up to us now . . . give it to 'em good!"

❧ Chapter 14 ❧

SAMUEL ADAMS LIVED for more than a quarter of a century after the American Revolution began. There was much work ahead for him before his dream of American independence would be fully realized. Yet his greatest task actually ended when that first musket shot reverberated through Lexington on April 19, 1775. It was true that, as more than one patriot soldier may well have remarked on that day, it was up to them now.

The battles that followed, all the way from Bunker Hill, Cowpens, Long Island, Trenton, Bennington, Saratoga, and the rest through to the final British surrender at Yorktown in October, 1781, would be won and lost by the Continental Army under its commander in chief, General George Washington. There was much more to winning the war than the battles, however. The American statesmen and members of the Continental Congress played essential roles in achieving victory. They had to perform the almost impossible task of raising money to feed, clothe, and arm the American soldiers in order to keep them fighting the well-equipped, experienced British forces. They also had to bolster the morale of the people, keeping them heartened and resolute through many dark days, when it seemed that the cause was lost. Not least of all they had to use all their persuasive powers in negotiating with the French to enlist their aid.

Nor did the first skirmishes on the green at Lexington and at Concord Bridge mean that the colonies were prepared to declare themselves independent. There were still many who believed that if they could settle their grievances with the Crown and establish their rights once and for all, it would be better to make peace and remain British subjects.

All of these things meant more work for Samuel Adams, and work he did, as faithfully and zealously as ever. But he was now joined by others who worked just as resolutely, men whose names, for one reason or another, were to become better known than his, Benjamin Franklin, Thomas Jefferson, John Adams, Robert Morris, and others.

It was Samuel Adams' dearest hope that the Continental Congress in Philadelphia would declare the American colonies free and independent as soon as possible. But when, in June, 1776, a committee was appointed to prepare a Declaration of Independence, it was John Adams, not Samuel, who was made one of the five members. And it was Thomas Jefferson who wrote the Declaration of Independence, though no better man could have been chosen to do it. It was not the kind of writing Samuel Adams could do well.

His role in American history rests upon the fact that he was more a politician and propagandist than a statesman. In the developments that took place during the 1776 meeting of the Continental Congress, the pattern of Samuel Adams' future began to form, a future less spectacular than his past.

His pen was just as facile, his way of speaking just as persuasive, and he used both to good advantage at the sessions of the Continental Congress at the State House, which people were beginning to call Independence Hall. He still put things pithily in a way that made people laugh. Some of the things he said were expressed with the sharp, terse humor that many years later made another New Englander famous, a Vermonter, President Calvin Coolidge.

One of them concerned General Horatio Gates' great victory when General John Burgoyne's British army surrendered at Saratoga in 1777. General Gates immediately sent his aide, James Wilkinson, to ride with all speed to York, Pennsylvania, where the Continental Congress was then meeting, to give the members the news.

Wilkinson was in love with a young lady from Philadelphia who was in nearby Reading at that time. Since he had not seen her for several months, he could not resist the temptation to stop there for a few minutes. The minutes stretched into hours, and before the young man knew it he was a whole day late. When he finally rode into York, news of the Saratoga victory had already preceded him.

Nevertheless, one of the members got up and said, "I move that the Congress express its gratitude to James Wilkinson, who has brought us this glorious news."

Samuel Adams rose, his expression grave, but with a humorous glint in his eye. "I move," he said, "that the Congress present the young gentleman with a pair of spurs."

When the Congress met he was always present, and he served on a number of its committees. Even when the British occupation of Philadelphia forced it to move to York, and its members were so disheartened by the Continental Army's defeats that only about twenty attended, Sam Adams was there.

At home, when the Congress was not in session, Samuel Adams had no spare moments. He had been elected Secretary of State of the Province of Massachusetts and was a delegate to the convention that drafted a constitution for the new state, the Commonwealth of Massachusetts.

In March, 1776, the siege of Boston ended, and Gage's British forces sailed away to New York. But if Samuel Adams expected to return to his old home on Purchase Street, he was quite wrong. It had been occupied by British officers, who had damaged it almost as much as the mob had once wrecked Thomas Hutchinson's mansion. Upon Adams' return from Philadelphia that summer, he found windows broken and doors torn from their hinges and burned for firewood. Furniture was falling apart; the walls were scrawled with caricatures and phrases offensive to the owner. Even the stable and other outbuildings had been destroyed and the garden wrecked. The place was no longer fit to live in, and regretfully Sam moved his family to Dedham, outside Boston.

About this time the friendship between Adams and John Hancock was broken off again, this time not to be resumed for ten years. After Hancock was named president of the Continental Congress, their relations became extremely bitter. Hancock, who had always enjoyed luxury and public acclaim, grew even more elegant and self-important in his new role. His conduct in general distressed both Sam and John Adams. Angered by their disapproval, Hancock withdrew his support of them in the Congress and made his action clear to the other delegates. This undoubtedly widened the breach between the two men who had worked side by side for the cause of liberty. Therefore it was a great blow to Sam that when Hancock gained political power in Boston, he offered his former friend no part in the molding of the future of Massachusetts.

In the early fall of 1780 the people thought well enough of Hancock to elect him the first governor of the new state. But when Sam Adams ran for Secretary of the Commonwealth a short time later, he was defeated. It humiliated him to find that his people were already beginning to forget him. Hancock, who had learned Sam's lessons all too well, was able to secure the leading position in Massachusetts, while Adams, who had bent all his efforts to bring about independence, could not gain even a lower post. Was that to be his final fate, he asked himself sadly.

In 1779 Adams' health was so poor that when he was again chosen as a delegate to the Continental Congress, he declined. His friends, however, insisted that he accept, and he did. Finally in November, 1780, he wrote Betsy from Philadelphia, "If I live till spring, I will take my final leave of Congress and return to Boston."

When spring came, the war was approaching its victorious end for America. Samuel Adams did resign as a delegate to Congress and return home. "I grow more domestic as I increase in years," he had written in the letter to Betsy, and he meant it. Nearly sixty now, he looked much older, for his hair was nearly white. And he was very tired.

Except for his devoted family, there was not much for him to come home to. He had no place of his own to live, nor even a job. However, the Massachusetts legislature permitted him to live in the confiscated house of a Tory, charging him a small rent. Betsy and Hannah came back from Dedham, and the family settled down in Boston again. Dr. Sam was not at home, for all through the war he was a surgeon with the Continental Army. Sam Adams managed to collect some money that had never been paid him for his services as clerk of the House of Representatives before Gage had prorogued it in 1774. So for a while, at least, the Adamses could get along.

The following year General Cornwallis surrendered, and the American Revolution was over. How often Samuel Adams must have dreamed of the day that would bring the greatest triumph of his life. Yet when it did come, the glory was not his. It belonged to General George Washington, his officers, the soldiers, and the members of the Continental Congress. Sam Adams was out of it. Perhaps he realized fully then that his own personal triumph had come six years earlier, on the green at Lexington.

In his famous poem, "Andrea del Sarto," Robert Browning wrote of a great artist who painted his masterpiece, a creation so perfect that the painter knew he could never again do one to equal it. After that, was there anything more to live for? His words, "Ah! but a man's reach should exceed his grasp, or what's a heaven for?" might very well have been Sam Adams' own. With the start of the Revolution his masterpiece was finished, and he could never create another like it.

Yet he could not admit that, even to himself. No man likes to think that his career is finished, his usefulness over. Politics was Samuel Adams' life. So back to politics he went, but mingled with the sweet taste of what he achieved there was much bitterness.

In 1781 he was elected to the State Senate, and its members chose him their president. He remained in that office until 1784, and in 1786 was elected to it again. It was an honor; yet all about him men whose abilities were inferior to his were rising to higher positions.

Not only John Hancock. When, in 1783, Samuel

Adams decided to run for lieutenant governor, he was beaten by Thomas Cushing, his long-time associate and friend. Cushing had been a patriot, true, but he had lacked Adams' determined will to fight for people's rights and liberties. In 1787, when Sam ran again, he was beaten by Benjamin Lincoln, who had been a Revolutionary general but not an outstanding one. In 1788 he ran for the United States Congress and lost to a young Boston lawyer.

A blow of another kind, even more heartbreaking, occurred that same year. After distinguished service in the Continental Army Dr. Sam had returned home, but he was not well. The hard life of the army camps and the long, bitter winters of the war years had shattered his health. At the age of only thirty-seven, he died.

Samuel Adams was grief-stricken. The two had always been very close. And although Sam needed no proof of his son's love, it was found when the young doctor's will was read. Like many another officer and soldier in the Revolution, he had not received a large part of the pay that was due him. And like the others, he had brought a claim against the government of the United States for the money. He left the claim to his father. When it was paid it amounted to twelve hundred pounds, or about four thousand dollars in United States currency.

In 1784 Sam had managed to buy a house on Winter Street in the South End of Boston. It was somewhat better than the family home on Purchase Street, but also old and rather dilapidated, its yellow paint faded and worn. It was the best he could afford, however. After his son's death, there were only Sam and Betsy at home. His daughter Hannah had married her step-mother's younger brother, Thomas Wells.

The long estrangement between Samuel Adams and John Hancock ended at last. For all John's faults, and Sam's, they had worked together too long for their quarrel to continue forever. For some time mutual friends tried to get them together, and finally they succeeded. In 1789, with Governor Hancock's support, Samuel Adams was elected lieutenant governor. It was the highest office he had ever held, but still not high enough for a man who had done so much for his country.

That same year, in New York City, John Adams, who had served with distinction as a statesman and minister to France and England after the war, was inaugurated Vice President of the United States. Sam did not begrudge his cousin that high office; they had long loved each other too well. However, the difference between the lieutenant governor of a state and the Vice President of the United States must have been painfully obvious to him.

Sam was to rise higher, but it was somehow like putting on the clothing of someone else who no longer had use for it. On October 8, 1793, John Hancock died, and Samuel Adams automatically succeeded him as governor. Now he occupied the highest office any man could attain in Massachusetts, but one thing bothered him; he wanted to be chosen for it by the people. The next year, when he ran for governor, his opponents, trying desperately to defeat him, claimed that he was too old. But the people of Massachusetts proved that they did not agree, even though he was over seventy, by electing him by a handsome majority.

In 1795 and 1796 they again re-elected him, and now Samuel Adams was satisfied. To be chosen governor three times had done much to heal the old wounds caused by the defeats he had suffered. His long experience in politics had enabled him to govern wisely and well. He had been an able chief executive, though not a brilliant one.

Perhaps he knew that history would not consider him a truly great governor of Massachusetts. The old fire was not there. The colonies had won their struggle for independence, and fighting for liberty was what he had done best and what made him great.

In 1797 Samuel Adams announced his retirement from public life. In that same year John Adams was inaugurated as the second President of the United States. Sam may have once dreamed of achieving such an honor, but he was seventy-five now and wanted to rest. At last he would be able to do so in the few years left to him.

It seems a miracle that Samuel Adams was able to spend those last years without any of the financial worries that had beset him almost all his life. And it is even more miraculous that Sam, who never had a whit of sense about money, should make a sound investment, but he did. With his inheritance from Dr. Sam he had bought a tavern and some other property in a suburb of Boston. With the substantial income that it brought in, plus the money he had saved during his years as governor of Massachusetts, he was not only able to live in comfort, but at the close of his life left sixteen thousand dollars.

Old friends often came to call upon him in his retirement, including many who came to Boston from other parts of the United States. Strangers to the house were apt to think its outside hardly befitted a former governor of Massachusetts. Once inside, however, they could not deny that Betsy was the best housekeeper in Boston, for the interior was spotless and beautifully kept.

The first floor was built low to the ground, so that a single step took a visitor up to the oak-paneled door with its big brass knocker. There they were admitted by Surry, now middle-aged, who had been the Adamses' servant for over thirty years. She had been a slave when a wealthy friend gave her to Betsy, but Samuel Adams, who detested slavery, had said, "A slave cannot live in my house. If she comes, she must be free." And free her he did.

Callers usually found the old patriot in his spacious sitting room library, surrounded by his many books. If the day was cool, a crackling fire sent out its warming heat, the leaping flames reflected in the quaint, blue-figured Dutch tiles that lined the front of the fireplace. The well-worn furniture had a homey, comfortable look. In one corner stood an ancient grandfather's clock that had belonged to Captain Samuel Adams. Two full-length oil paintings of Sam and Betsy added further personal charm to the room.

If Sam was reading, he would be wearing spectacles but would remove them as he rose to greet his visitor. To the end of his life he needed glasses only for writing and reading. And although almost from the time he entered politics he had looked older than his years, in his old age he looked younger, for his face had few wrinkles.

Those who met him for the first time were impressed by what they saw. In his long life Samuel Adams had gained a broad knowledge of people. He knew their faults; yet he was aware that there was good in the worst of them, and this knowledge had lent kindliness to the strength of his face. It was a careworn face, but there was serenity in the blue eyes set in a ruddy complexion under the heavy eyebrows. And although the tremor in his hands and voice was very noticeable now, it did not affect the great dignity that had always been his.

Samuel Adams often walked about Boston in those last years, but it was a very different town now. Cornhill had become Washington Street. King Street was State. The old State House was still there, as it is today, but on Beacon Hill, in what had once been John Hancock's pasture, stood the magnificent new State House with its huge, copper-sheathed dome.

And there were many other changes in people, too. On his walks Samuel Adams passed young people who had not even been born when the Revolution began. To the boys and girls he met on their way to or from school, the Stamp Act, the Townshend Act, and the Boston Massacre were dull dates to be learned from a textbook. To them it did not seem that such things as the Boston Tea Party had really happened. He, Samuel Adams, was in those books, too, but the children he passed did not recognize the old gentleman in the red cloak, with his tiewig, cocked hat, buckled shoes, and knee breeches.

Some people still remembered, however. The few patriots and Sons of Liberty who were still alive recognized that familiar figure and would stop and chat with him. *They* knew that the history in the textbooks was real.

Best of all, so did Sam's family. He found his greatest contentment at home. Nothing could fill the vacant place his son's death had left, of course. And old Queue, the canine patriot, had long since ceased to chase redcoats or lie at his master's feet. But there was Betsy, always loyal and devoted, who had stood by Sam through the long, tempestuous, poverty-stricken years. She was still at his side to make his last days comfortable and happy with her loving care. And Hannah, who had once been awed that her father would write a letter to King George III, was often at the house on Winter Street with her husband and her daughter and sons. Sam's grandchildren remained a constant source of pleasure to the old man.

The year 1800 came, the birth of a new century, then 1802 and Sam's eightieth birthday. His steps were very slow and feeble now. He walked mostly in his garden, or a few paces up and down the street in front of the house.

Another year passed. On the night of October 1, Samuel Adams' breathing grew difficult, and he slept only a few hours. Early the next morning, October 2, 1803, his family and a few close friends were summoned to his bedside. Dawn came, and he was sleeping, but at seven o'clock he stirred restlessly and uttered a few whispered words. Hannah, who was closest to his bed, leaned forward but was unable to make out what he said.

Then the spark of life within Samuel Adams, the great patriot who had been called the Chief Incendiary because he had lighted and tended untiringly the fire that finally flamed into the American Revolution, flickered out.

Bibliography

Appolonio, Thornton D. *Boston Public Schools, Past and Present*. Boston: Wright & Potter, 1923.

Bevis, A. M. *Diets and Riots, an Interpretation of the History of Harvard*. Boston: Marshall Jones Co., 1936.

Blaney, Henry R. *Old Boston*. Boston: Lee & Shepard, 1896.

Bowen, Catherine Drinker. *John Adams and the American Revolution*. Boston: Little, Brown & Co., 1950.

Brayley, Arthur Wellington. *Schools and Schoolboys of Old Boston*. Boston: Louis P. Hager, 1894.

Bush, George Gary. *Harvard, the First American University*. Boston: Cupples, Upham & Co., 1886.

Catalogue of the Masters and Scholars Who Have Belonged to the Public Latin School, Boston, Mass., from 1635 to 1879. Boston: Boston Latin School Association, 1878.

Crawford, Mary Caroline. *Social Life in Old New England*. New York: Grosset & Dunlap, 1914.

Cunningham, Henry Winchester (ed.). *Diary of the Rev. Samuel Checkley*. Cambridge: John Wilson & Sons, 1909.

Cushing, Henry Alonzo (ed.). *Writings of Samuel Adams*. New York: G. P. Putnam's Sons, 1904.

Davis, Andrew McFarland. "Boston Banks, 1681-1740." *New England Historical and Genealogical Register*, July, 1903.

———. *Currency and Banking in the Province of the Massachusetts Bay.* Publications of the American Economic Association, Series 3, Vol. 1, No. 4, and Vol. 2, No. 2.

Deane, Charles (ed.). *Tutor Henry Flynt's Journey from Cambridge to Portsmouth in 1754.* Cambridge: John Wilson & Sons, 1878.

Drake, Francis S. *Tea Leaves, Being a Collection of Letters and Documents Relating to the Shipment of Tea to the American Colonies in the Year 1773, by the East India Tea Company.* Boston: A. O. Crane, 1884.

Drake, Samuel Adams. *Old Landmarks of Boston.* Boston: James R. Osgood & Co., 1875.

———. *The History and Antiquities of Boston.* Boston: Luther Stevens, 1884.

Earle, Alice Morse. *Child Life in Colonial Days.* New York: Macmillan Co., 1899.

———. *Home Life in Colonial Days.* New York: Grosset & Dunlap, 1898.

Forbes, Esther. *Paul Revere and the World He Lived In.* Boston: Houghton Mifflin Co., 1942.

French, Allen. *Day of Concord and Lexington.* Boston: Little, Brown & Co., 1925.

———. *Old Concord.* Boston: Little, Brown & Co., 1915.

Hart, Albert Bushnell (ed.). *Commonwealth History of Massachusetts.* New York: States History Co., 1930.

Historical Register of Harvard University, 1636-1936. Cambridge: Harvard University Press, 1937.

Holmes, Pauline. *Tercentenary History of the Boston Public Latin School, 1635-1935.* Cambridge: Harvard University Press, 1935.

Hosmer, James K. *American Statesmen—Samuel Adams.* Boston: Houghton Mifflin Co., 1885.

Lovett, James D'Wolfe. *Old Boston Boys and the Games They Played*. Boston: Riverside Press, 1906.

Matthews, Albert. "Harvard Commencement Days, 1642-1916." *Publication of the Colonial Society of Massachusetts*, Boston: Vol. XVIII.

———."Notes on 'Placing' at Harvard College," *ibid.*, Vol. XXV.

Miller, John C. *Origins of the American Revolution*. Boston: Little, Brown & Co., 1943.

———. *Samuel Adams, Pioneer In Propaganda*. Stanford, Calif.: Stanford University Press, 1960.

Morison, Samuel Adams. *Three Centuries of Harvard, 1636-1936*. Cambridge: Harvard University Press, 1936.

Peirce, Benjamin. *History of Harvard University*. Cambridge: Shattuck & Co., 1833.

Pier, Arthur Stanwood. *Story of Harvard*. Boston: Little, Brown & Co., 1913.

Publications on ropewalks. Plymouth Cordage Co.

Quincy, Josiah. *History of Harvard University*. Cambridge: John Owen, 1840.

Ridpath, John Clark. *James Otis, the Pre-Revolutionist*. Milwaukee: H. G. Campbell Publishing Co., 1903.

Scudder, Townsend. *Concord, American Town*. Boston: Little, Brown & Co., 1947.

Seybolt, Robert Francis. *Public Schools of Colonial Boston, 1635-1775*. Cambridge: Harvard University Press, 1935.

Shurtleff, Nathaniel. *Topographical and Historical Description of Boston*. Boston: City Council of Boston, 1871.

Sparks, Jared. *Library of American Biography—James Otis,* Vol. XII. Boston: Charles C. Little & James Brown, 1884.

Stark, James H. *Antique Views of Ye Towne of Boston.* Boston: Photo-Electrotype Engraving Co., 1882.

Thayer, William R. "Historical Sketch of Harvard University," *History of Middlesex County, Massachusetts.* Cambridge: Privately published: 1890.

Tudor, William. *Life of James Otis of Massachusetts.* Boston: Wells & Lilly Co., 1823.

Two Hundred and Fiftieth Anniversary of Harvard College. Cambridge: Shepard Memorial Church, 1887.

Wadsworth, Benjamin. "Benjamin Wadsworth's Book (A. Dom. 1725)," *Publication of the Colonial Society of Massachusetts,* Vol. XXXI, 1935.

Wagner, Charles A. *Harvard, Four Centuries and Freedoms.* New York: E. P. Dutton & Co., 1950.

Wells, William V. *Life and Public Services of Samuel Adams.* Boston: Little, Brown & Co., 1865.

Winsor, Justin (ed.). *Memorial History of Boston, 1630-1880.* Boston: James R. Osgood & Co., 1881.

❧ Index ❧

About the Author

CLIFFORD LINDSEY ALDERMAN has written three novels, is at work on a fourth, and has two biographies for young people to his credit. His great interest is eighteenth-century New England, and he feels that Samuel Adams was one of the era's most outstanding characters.

Mr. Alderman was graduated from the Naval Academy at Annapolis, but did not remain in the Naval service. After a summer as fourth officer of the liner *Siboney,* on the New York-Havana run, he entered M.I.T. for postgraduate work. In 1942, he returned to the Navy as lieutenant commander, and taught officer candidates at Holy Cross, Millsaps, and Middlebury colleges, and Columbia University.

He has done public-relations work, edited several magazines, and has published in many more. He now devotes his time entirely to writing. With his wife, he has traveled through Europe, the West Indies, Canada, and the United States.